Wild Roses

And

Childhood Memories

A Cookbook Written by
Marlo Ann

Magic Valley
Publishers

Sale of this book without a front cover may be unauthorized. If this book is without a cover, it may have been reported to the publisher as "unsold or destroyed" and neither the author nor the publisher may have received payment for it.

Published by Magic Valley Publishers
Copyright 2006 © by Marlo A Smith
All Rights Reserved.

Except for use in any review, the reproduction of this work in whole or in part in any form by any electronic, mechanical or other means, now known or hereafter invented, including xerography, photocopying and recording, or in any information storage or retrieval system, is forbidden without the written permission of the publisher, Magic Valley Publishers, 6390 E Willow St, Long Beach CA 90815 U.S.A.

ISBN 0-9785509-4-3
Cover design by Shelby Lydon

Manufactured in the United States of America

First Edition

I wish to dedicate this book, as a tribute, to my Mom. She was a wonderful mom and an amazing woman. We all loved her dearly and miss her. She could do anything; I could fill a book about her. Amongst her talents, she could cook and bake better than anyone!

Wild Roses and Childhood Memories

FOREWORD

This is a cookbook that I have been thinking about for over fifteen years. It is time the thinking becomes a reality, as the memory fades and time slips away.

My childhood was on a farm in Indiana. I had five brothers and lots of boy cousins, in fact there were no other little girls around. It was keep up with the boys or be by myself, needless to say, I was a tomboy. Now my Mom had other ideas, she wanted a girl! Although she sheltered me from the heavy farm work, I certainly had my share of the chores. There was some field work but mostly it was doing the wash, hanging the clothes on the line, taking them down, ironing, cleaning, cooking, gardening and taking care of my little brothers. Of course we all had fun when we played cowboys and Indians, softball and basketball, tag and all those fun things kids did before the electronic age.

One problem I found, in preparing to put these recipes in a book, is many had never been written down. Her old cookbooks have gotten lost over the years. Mom taught me how to cook by using what ingredients we had, what went well together and how to add a pinch of this and a little of that. So, I have had to prepare dishes, with pen and paper in hand to write down what all goes in it and measure how much. Some she had sent to me in letters over the years. The foods of our family and friends bring back the many happy memories of childhood.

MY RECIPE BOX

Going through my recipe box has brought back so many memories. The box itself was made for me by my father-in-law, who was like a father to me and we miss him. I was very fortunate to have married into a second set of loving parents. I appreciate both sets of parents and what they have taught me.

Me and my brother Gene

The hand written recipes from my daughters mean so much. Time flashes back as I see those little heads bobbing in and out the door. As I recall the stages from babies to toddlers, just starting school, becoming teenagers, young adults, and finally marriages with families of their own, I find great joy watching the grandchildren going through the same circle of life.

When I was young, I always wanted to do something important, something to be remembered by, to travel, to write some great novel, something. As I have gotten older and still have these desires, I thought I had better get busy with my ambitions. One day it came to me; I had already done it, something important to be remembered by. I have given birth to four wonderful daughters. What better gift could I give to the world?

Kathy, Debbie, Lisa, Laurie

Our four lovely daughters are now successful working Mothers with careers. Their children, our nine grandchildren, are young adults working on their careers.

I hope you enjoy the recipes. Some are old with much effort to prepare, but, it lets us remember the days before we had TV dinners (or TV) and prepackaged meals. We can appreciate our Mothers before us and the work it took to prepare the family meal. We sat around the kitchen table and ate together as a family.

Contents

APPETIZERS AND DIPS   **18**
Spinach Dip
Whole Roasted Garlic
Artichoke Dip
Deviled Eggs
Pickled Eggs

BREADS   **21**
Banana Nut Bread
Banana Nut Oatmeal Muffins
Banana Bread
Pumpkin Bread
Cranberry Bread
Zucchini Bread
Chocolate Zucchini Bread
Zucchini Loaf
Gingerbread
Cornbread

DESSERTS   **54**
Fruit Cobbler
Date Bars
Lemon Bars
Brownies
7 Layer Bars
Mincemeat Bars
Heavenly Delight

COOKIES   **30**
Everything Cookie
Chocolate Chip Cookies
Sour Cream Sugar Cookies with Frosting
Peanut Butter Cookies
Sugar Cookies
Crisscrossed Peanut Butter Cookies
Oatmeal Cookies
Pineapple Cookies
Cocoanut Cookies

CANDY   **37**
Penoche
Hershey Fudge
Microwave Fudge
Microwave Peanut Brittle
Divinity

Fruity Candy
Chewy Sesame Candy
Microwave Rice Crispy Candy
Rice Crispy Marshmallow Squares
Fantasy Fudge
See's Fudge

CAKES 42
Fruit Cocktail Cake with Frosting
Carrot Cake with Frosting
Wine Cake
Laurie's Applesauce Cake
Black Walnut or Hickory Nut Cake
Sauerkraut Cake with Mocha Frosting
Italian Cream Cake with Cream Cheese Frosting
Fruit Cake
Chocolate Red Devils Food Cake
Devils Food Cake

FROSTINGS 51
Powdered Sugar Frosting
Butter Cream Frosting
Cream Cheese Frosting
Mocha Cream
Italian Cream Cake Frosting
Basic Butter Cream Frosting & variations
No Cook Marshmallow Frosting
Marshmallow Icing
Satiny Icing
* Some frostings are with cake recipe

CHEESECAKE 53
Pineapple Cheesecake
Cherry Cheesecake

MORE DESSERTS 54
Tapioca Pudding
Zella's Dessert
Pineapple Upside Down Cake
Éclairs & Creampuffs

APPLES 58
Apple Dumplins
Apple Raisin Crunch
Apple Crisp
Baked Apples

PIES 62
Chocolate Pie
Mom's Cream Pie Fillings
Lemon Pie
Mincemeat
Mincemeat Pie
Tomato Pie
My Pecan Pie
Pecan Pie
Rosy Red Rhubarb Cake (like Pie)
Strawberry Pie

PIE CRUSTS 72
Apple Pie
Fresh Peach Pie
Blueberry or Blackberry Pie
Cherry Pie
Perfect Pumpkin Pie
Famous Pumpkin Pie
More Pie Crusts
Nancy's Pie Crust
Graham Cracker Crust

SALADS & DRESSINGS 74
Potato Salad
Broccoli Salad
Spinach & Strawberry Salad
Tavern Dressing
Mandarin Orange Spinach Salad
Crunchy Pea Salad
Avocado & Grapefruit Salad
Hot Potato Salad
Oriental Salad
Country Salad
Celery Seed Dressing
Dandelion Greens Salad
Cranberry Orange Relish
Tomato Cheese Salad
Raspberry Salad

SOUPS 83
Vegetable Soup
Minestrone Soup

Pea Soup
French Onion Soup
Beef & Barley Soup

NOODLES 86
Noodle Soup
Potato Soup with Ruffles
Milk Soup

MAIN DISHES 91
Cabbage Rolls
Farmer Style Spareribs
Chili Mac
Goop
Pizza and Crust
Spaghetti Sauce
Meat Loaf
Lasagna
Green Bean Casserole
Sweet Potatoes
Beef Stew
Potato Pancakes
Mashed Potato Pancakes
Gulliver's Corn
Ron's Meatloaf
Sweet & Sour Pork
Zucchini & Cheese
Zucchini & Tomatoes
Zucchini & Velvetta Cheese
Hot Dog Casserole
Tuna Boats
Camper Stew
Chili Reljeno
Classic Chicken Divan
Chicken & Olive DeVille

MEXICAN FOOD 108
Tacos
Enchiladas
Fish Tacos

JELLY AND JAMS 113
 Tomato preserves
Apricot Jam
Blackberry Jam
Strawberry Fig Jam

BEVERAGES 117
Sun Tea
Russian Tea
Mint Tea
Wassail
Brandy Alexander
Mexican Chocolate

SEAFOOD 120
Shrimp
Tartar Sauces

BAKING AND SUBSTITUTIONS

Those days we had to use cake flour instead of regular flour to bake, as the chemistry is different. I have listed some of the substitutions that you can use or may be necessary to use. I often find when I start to make something that there is always one ingredient that I do not have.

1. Flour - When baking a cake from scratch (not a cake mix) one should use Cake Flour, unless the recipe calls for All Purpose Flour. Cake flour is a soft wheat flour that contains less gluten than all purpose or bread flour. It goes through a special milling process. It gives a finer texture to the cake. If it is necessary to substitute all purpose flour for cake flour, use two tablespoons less per cup than what the recipe calls for. The texture results will not be as fine as with cake flour. Sift the flour once before measuring. Flour should not be packed down. Sifting eliminates packing. Sift into a bowl and lightly place into measuring cup or the nesting cups. Do not shake. After flour is sifted and measured, put back in the sifter along with any salt, leavening or spices and sift together in recipe at appropriate time. This can be sifted again to make a finer texture.

2. Leavening - It is what causes the chemical reaction that makes the cake or bread rise. Leavening agents are Baking Powder, Baking Soda and Cream of Tartar, also beaten egg whites. In sponge and angel food cakes, air is beaten into eggs or egg whites and is usually the only leavening. Baking soda is used when the liquid is sour cream, sour milk or buttermilk, also when molasses is in the recipe. Cream of tartar is used when egg whites are beaten separately and folded into batter, example is Angel Food Cake.

3. Granulated Sugar does not pack like flour so it does not have to be sifted. Do not shake it down to get a level cup. Brown sugar needs to be packed down as it is moist, unless the recipe states otherwise, which would be rare. The chemistry of the leavening action determines the type of leavening used, also why measurements are so important when baking a cake.

4. Sour Milk is used, especially in older recipes or those used by folks who bought un-pasteurized milk and before there was homogenized milk. So there is a difference between sour milk and spoiled milk. In today's world if I was making an old recipe that called for sour milk, I would take one Tablespoon of plain cider vinegar and put in a cup of sweet milk and that will make sour milk. If it calls for sour cream, that is available at the grocery store. Some recipes give you an option of sour milk or buttermilk. It is the chemical reaction you want, so either would do. If one wanted to experiment and use buttermilk in recipes that called for sour milk and does not specify, that is part of the fun of cooking. Recipes are guides to go by. At least that is my opinion.

GARDENS

We always had a small garden and a large one called a truck patch. The small one had the normal table vegetables, like green onions, peas, lettuce radishes and so forth. The *truck garden* was the one we grew the vegetables to can. Mom preserved (canned) our vegetables for the winter months. We grew green beans, tomatoes, cabbage, carrots, potatoes, bell peppers, hot peppers, pickles, watermelon, cantaloupe or musk melon, corn and I am sure many others. The cabbage was used as coleslaw, cooked cabbage or roasted with pot roast, but the hard work was making sauerkraut.

We had to grate the cabbage and then pickle it in large crocks and then she canned it in quart jars. My Dad would buy a truck load of bushels of peaches. He could sell enough of them to off set the fuel cost, as he would drive up to Michigan where there were many peach orchards. My brothers and I would have to peel peaches by the bushels, which wasn't too bad. When Dad came home with boxes and boxes of cherries, we had to pit those cherries and the only redeeming factor was thinking about all the cherry pies they would make. We were happy when they were Bing cherries as we didn't have to pit them. My Mom had to carry the water from the well, wash all the jars and prepare all the food in them and use various means to preserve them, on a cook stove in the kitchen. I can remember the times when she would have the jars in the pressure cooker on the stove. We had to sit and watch the time and the temperature on the cooker, as she had to go out and milk the cows and do the animal chores. There were times when we would forget and then see the temperature up high and climbing, run out to the barn to say to Mom "What do we do now?" She always (usually) was very patient and told us what we needed to do. I wish I could repay her for all the love and lessons she taught us.

Our basement had hundreds of jars of food for the winter. We were not allowed to waste our food. We counted our blessings.

My Mom in the garden

Appetizers and Dips

Deviled Eggs

Breads

Making raised yeast breads from scratch has never been a very successful endeavor for me. So when bread machines came out, I had one. Even then, rarely was I happy with the bread. So I have not included any of the recipes my Mom or any of the family and friends have passed on to me. I do have some wonderful bread recipes. These recipes that have been included have been tried many times and are very good. The banana breads have been passed around the family and it is one of our favorites, These breads are all very good, make nice gifts at the holidays or welcome to the neighborhood. Yes, we still do that. There is nothing like a good loaf of homemade bread to make a friend , share with a friend, or just have with the ones you love, along with a cup of coffee or tea.

If I have bananas that are getting overripe, I peel them and put in a sealed up plastic bag or Tupperware type of container, and freeze. When I am in the mood to make Banana bread, I have bananas to use.

To check for doneness in these breads, use the toothpick method. Stick a toothpick upright in the middle of the loaf or muffin tin, or cake pan, this is a good test on most cakes. If the toothpick comes out clean, the bread or cake is done. If mixture sticks to toothpick, cook a little longer.

Banana Nut Bread with Pistachio

Marlo Ann

BANANA NUT BREAD

½ cup cooking oil
1 cup sugar
2 eggs beaten (can beat in a
Small bowl with a fork)
3 ripe bananas, mashed.
3 Tbsp milk
½ tsp vanilla

2 cups all purpose flour
1 tsp Baking soda
½ tsp Baking Powder
½ tsp salt
½ cup chopped nuts

If preferred you can add ½ cup raisins or other dried fruit

Beat the oil and sugar together well. (Use mixer or large spoon). Add the beaten eggs and bananas. Beat well. Sift and add the dry ingredients alternately with the milk and vanilla. Mix well and stir in nuts (and other fruits if you choose to add)
Pour into greased and floured loaf pan 9x5x3 for about 1 hour.
350degrees. Or you can make muffins, bake 20 to 25 minutes

BANANA NUT BRAN-OATMEAL MUFFINS

½ cup cooking oil
¾ cup honey
2 eggs (beaten)
3 ripe mashed bananas
3 Tbsp milk

2 cups all purpose flour
½ cup oatmeal
¼ cup wheat bran
½ tsp Baking Powder
1 tsp Baking Soda

½ cup nuts (raisins are also good added)

Beat oil and honey, add eggs stir, add bananas. Beat well.
Sift and add dry ingredients alternately with flour & vanilla.
Add nuts (and raisins). Pour into greased muffin tins or loaf pan, 9x5x3 for approx. 1 hour 350 degrees, muffins 20 to 25 minutes.

BANANA BREAD

1 ¾ cup flour
2 tsp baking powder
¾ tsp salt
¾ cup sugar

2 eggs
1 cup (3 med ripe mashed
  bananas)
1/3 cup oil

1. Sift flour, baking powder, sugar & salt.
2. Beat eggs and bananas and oil
3. Mix liquid & dry mixture can add ½ cup nuts if desired
   Stir do not beat.
4. Pour into greased loaf pan. Bake 350 for approx 1 hr.

PUMPKIN BREAD

1 cup white sugar	2 cups flour All Purpose
½ cup brown sugar, packed	1 tsp. Baking soda
1 cup pumpkin (canned)	½ tsp salt
½ cup salad oil	½ tsp nutmeg
2 eggs unbeaten	½ tsp cinnamon
½ cup chopped nuts	1 tsp ginger
¾ cups raisins	¼ cup water

Combine sugars, pumpkin, oil and eggs. Beat until blended. Sift & add flour, soda, salt and spices to pumpkin mixture and mix well. Add raisins, nuts and water, mix, pour into well greased 9x5x3 loaf pan. Bake 60 min. at 350 degrees or till done. Cool before cutting. Can turn over on a rack to cool.

CRANBERRY BREAD

This was made by Christina and she brought it to our Christmas gathering, it was so delicious, it is going to be a regular Holiday treat. We have had it the past two years at Christmas time.

2 cups all purpose flour	¼ cup butter
1 cup white sugar	1 egg
1 ½ tsp baking Powder	¾ cup orange juice
1 tsp salt	1 Tbsp grated orange peel (zest)
½ tsp Baking soda	1 ½ cups fresh or frozen Cranberries
	½ cup chopped Walnuts

1. Preheat over to 350. Lightly grease one loaf pan
2. Mix together flour, sugar, Baking powder, Baking soda. Cut in butter until mixture resembles small crumbs.
3. In a small bowl beat egg, orange juice and orange zest. Blend into dry ingredients. Stir in cranberries and walnuts. Put in pan.
4. Bake in preheated oven 65 to 70 Min. Do the toothpick test to see if it comes out clean, which means it is done. Cool 10 min.

ZUCCHINI BREAD

1 egg	1 cup flour
2/3 cup white sugar	¼ Tsp Baking soda
1/3 cup salad oil	1/8 Tsp Baking powder
2/3 cup raw zucchini grated	¼ tsp salt
1 tsp. Vanilla	

Preheat oven to 350 degrees. In a mixing bowl, mix sugar, oil and egg, add zucchini, vanilla and mix well. Sift the flour, baking soda and powder and salt, add to the zucchini and mix well. Pour into a loaf pan and bake 50 minutes

Marlo Ann

CHOCOLATE ZUCCHINI BREAD

3 cups all purpose flour	3 cups white sugar
½ cup cocoa	1 ½ cups salad oil
1 ½ tsp Baking Powder	4 eggs
1 ½ tsp Baking Soda	2 Tbsp margarine
1 tsp salt	1 ½ tsp vanilla
¼ tsp cinnamon	3 cups grated raw Zucchini
1 cup raisins	1 cup chopped pecans

In mixing bowl sift together the flour, baking soda, baking powder, salt and cinnamon, set aside. In a mixing bowl, beat together the sugar, oil, margarine and eggs. Add the vanilla and the zucchini, mixing well. Stir in the dry ingredients and mix well, Add nuts and raisins, mix and pour into a greased 8 x 4 x2 inch pan. Bake in preheated 350 degree oven 1 hour, or till done, cool before cutting. I have used a 9 x 5 x3 inch pan also.

The previous two zucchini recipes were given to me by my neighbor and dear friend, Ione.

ZUCCHINI LOAF

1 ½ cups all purpose flour	1 cup white sugar
1 tsp cinnamon	1 egg
½ tsp baking soda	¼ cup vegetable oil
½ tsp salt	¼ tsp. finely grated lemon peel
½ tsp nutmeg'	1 cup finely grated raw unpeeled zucchini
¼ tsp baking powder	

Heat over to 350 degrees. In a mixing bowl sift together flour, cinnamon, baking soda, salt, nutmeg and baking powder, set aside. In a mixing bowl beat together sugar zucchini and egg. Add oil and lemon peel, mix well. Stir in flour mixture to zucchini mixture and stir well. Pour into a greased 8x4x2 loaf pan or a 9x5x3 if that is what is available to you. Bake at 350 degree preheated oven for approx one hour. Check with toothpick at 55 minutes. Prep time approx 15 min. plus bake time. Cool before cutting.

Marlo Ann and little brother Kenny, big brother Gene

GINGERBREAD

1 ½ cups all purpose flour or   1/3 cup soft margarine
    (1 2/3 cups cake flour)   ½ cup sugar
¼ tsp salt   1 egg
½ tsp soda   ½ cup light molasses
½ tsp cinnamon   ½ cup buttermilk
1 tsp ginger

    Sift flour and resift 3 times with salt, soda and spices. (Only if you use all purpose flour. Cake flour only sift together once.) Cream margarine until smooth, add sugar and egg, cream until light and fluffy. Add molasses and beat vigorously for 2 minutes longer. Add flour mixture alternately with buttermilk, 3 or 4 portions. Begin and end with flour. Beat well after each addition. Pour batter into a greased 11/7/1 ½ inch pan. Bake 350 degrees for 25 to 30 minutes. Cool. Serve warm or cold with whipped cream.

CORNBREAD

1 Cup ground corn meal   1/3 cup shortening
1 Cup flour   1 egg
2 Tbsp sugar (more can be added)   1 cup milk
1 Tbsp Baking Powder
1 Tsp salt

Combine dry ingredients in bowl, mix well. If a sweeter cornbread is desired another Tbsp can be added. Cut in shortening until well blended. Add egg, slightly beaten and milk, mixing until just blended. Bake in oven at 400 degree for 25 min. in 8" square pan.

FRUIT COBBLER

½ Cup butter or margarine
1 cup milk
1 cup sugar
1 cup flour
1 tsp baking powder
1 tsp. vanilla
4 cups fruit (any fresh fruit in season, especially good for black berries, peaches and apricots)

Melt margarine in a 9 x13 "pan. Mix milk, sugar, flour, vanilla and baking powder together in the pan. Spoon fruit over the batter. Bake 350 degrees for 1 hour. Great with vanilla ice cream or whipped cream.

I have tried many cobblers and this is my choice to make. It is easy, simple and very good.

DATE BARS

¼ cup butter or margarine   1 1/3 cup Bisquick
¾ cup white sugar   ½ cup chopped nut (walnuts)
1 egg   1 cup chopped up dates

Heat oven to 350 degrees. Mix butter, sugar & egg thoroughly. Stir in Bisquick, nuts and dates. Bake 20 minutes in greased 8" square pan. Cool about 1 hr., cut in bars, roll in powdered sugar.
Recipe can be doubled. They go fast. Don't over bake as they become dry and are best just a little under baked.

LEMON BARS

Crust
¼ lb. Butter (room temp)
¼ cup powdered sugar
1 cup flour
Pinch of salt
Mix ingredients well and pat into a greased 9X9" square pan.
Bake 350 degrees for 25 minutes

Filling
2 eggs   1 cup sugar
½ tsp baking powder   2 Tbsp flour
Juice and grated rind of 2 lemons
Beat all the ingredients well. Pour over hot crust. Bake at 350 degrees 20 to 25 minutes. Sprinkle with powdered sugar when slightly cool. Cut into squares and enjoy.

My daughter, Kathy, gave me this recipe years ago and it is one of our favorites.

Peach and Berry Cobbler with Ice Cream

Wild Roses and Childhood Memories

GREENIES OR GREEN BROWNIES

There is a family legend that I have hear about ever since I have known my husband, Ron and his parents   This is a span of over fifty years. It seems when Ron was a youngster, he made a pan of Brownies and added green food coloring, making them green brownies. These were the best brownies that he or his parents had ever eaten in their whole lives. Unfortunately, no one knows what he put in those brownies, so only the memories of them remain.   I cannot provide you with a recipe for Greenies, I can only do the next best, with the basic Brownie recipe below. (Maybe you can add the green food coloring and imagine Greenies)

BROWNIES

Beat 2 eggs   low speed 1 minute and gradually add
1 cup sugar   beat med speed 1 minute

Mix together 1/3 cup melted butter
              2 squares of melted chocolate
Add to the sugar mixture and beat 1 minute on med. Speed

Sift together ¾ cups cake flour
              ½ tsp baking powder
              ¼ tsp salt
Add to chocolate mixture
              ½ cups chopped nuts
               1 tsp vanilla
Mix together and pour into 8" square baking pan
Bake at 325 degrees for 25 minutes
Cut in squares while warm, cool. They can be frosted with chocolate powdered sugar frosting.

SEVEN LAYER BARS

(Kathy gave me this recipe and it is great for a party or group)

½ cup butter or margarine
1 ½ cups finely crushed graham crackers
1 Package 6 oz. size (1 cup) chocolate chips
1 Package 6 oz. size (1 cup) butterscotch chips
1 1/3 cups flaked cocoanut
½ cups chopped walnuts
1 (14 oz can) 1- 1/3 cup sweetened condensed milk

Melt butter, stir in graham crackers. Pat crumb mixture evenly in bottom of ungreased
13 X 9 ½" baking pan
Layer in order the chocolate chips, butterscotch chips, cocoanut and walnuts.
Pour sweetened condensed milk evenly over all.
Bake at 350 degrees for 30 minutes. Cool and cut into bars.

MINCEMEAT BARS

2 ½ cups Bisquick
1 cup sugar
1 egg
3 Tbsp butter
¼ cup milk
1 ½ cups of mincemeat

Heat oven to 375 degrees. Mix all the above ingredients except mincemeat. Pat half of dough into greased 13 x9" pan, within ½ inch of the edge. Spread with the mincemeat. Pat out other half of dough on piece of waxed paper, turn over on top of the mincemeat. Remove paper. Bake 30 minutes. When cool, frost with thin powdered sugar frosting.

HEAVENLY DELIGHT
(Sex In a Pan) intriguing name

Requires a 9 X 13 Glass baking dish

1st layer
　　　1 cup flour
　　　1 cube margarine
　　　1 cup finely chopped walnuts of pecans
Mix margarine & flour as you would for a pie crust. Add nuts. Press dough in the bottom of the pan (don't go up the sides) for the crust. Bake at 350 degrees for 20 to 25 minutes. Let completely cool.

2nd layer
　　　Whip 1 (8 oz) package of Philadelphia Cream cheese, add 1 cup powdered sugar. Mix Well. Gently add ½ of a 16 oz. Container of Cool Whip. Spread over 1st layer

3rd layer
　　　3 cups milk
　　　1 small box instant chocolate pudding
　　　1 small box instant vanilla pudding
Mix all three ingredients together in a bowl until thick. Spread over 2nd layer.

4th layer
　　　Spread remainder of Cool Whip over 3rd layer.
Finely grate a Large size Hershey Bar and cover the Cool Whip with it and some chopped nuts. Keep refrigerated until serving.

Because it is so rich, cut into small bar size.
This is a good dessert for a large group.

One can relax in my yard

Cookies

Everyone loves cookies and there are so many recipes, variations and I have only selected the very favorites. I have many that have not been made for years and are similar to others. I hope you enjoy trying these and especially eating them.

We have some very dear friends, Charles and Sharon Billings, they live in Washington. These are the greatest people ever and we feel very privileged to have them as friends. Sharon tries many different recipes and is a great cook. We always look forward to one of her meals as they are delicious. When we were served her cookies, we loved them. I requested the recipe… I call it a Health Cookie but she calls it EVERYTHING COOKIE

In the fall it is baking cookie time. The orange flowers (yes they are flowers) are Chinese lanterns from my yard

EVERYTHING COOKIE

1 Cup butter or margarine	2 cups flour
1 cup granulated sugar	1 tsp baking soda
1 cup packed brown sugar	½ tsp baking powder
2 eggs	¼ tsp salt
1 tsp vanilla	1 cup chocolate chips
2 cups oatmeal	½ cup chopped nuts
2 cups corn flakes	½ cup raisins
½ cup flaked cocoanut	½ cup dried cranberries

Preheat oven to 350 degrees. Cream butter and sugar until creamy. Add eggs and vanilla. Beat well. Combine flour, baking soda, baking powder and salt, then add to wet ingredients and mix well.
Stir in rest of ingredients and mix well. Drop by heaping tablespoons on un greased cookie sheet. Bake 10 to 12 minutes (until very lightly browned) Allow to cool one minute on cookie sheet before removing. Store tightly covered.

CHOCOLATE CHIP COOKIES

2 ¼ cup all purpose flour
1 tsp baking soda
½ tsp salt
¾ cup packed brown sugar
¾ cup granulated sugar
1 cup softened butter or margarine (2 sticks)
2 eggs
3 cups chocolate chips
1 cup chopped nuts

Combine flour, soda and salt in small bowl. Beat the butter and sugars and vanilla in large bowl with mixer for two minutes on med. Speed. Then add eggs one at a time and beat in between. Gradually beat in the flour mixture. Gradually stir in the flour mixture and beat together well Add the chocolate chips and nuts, stir till mixed. Drop by Tbsp on un- greased cookie sheets.

Bake in preheated 350 oven for 8 to 9 minutes, just until a light golden brown. A little under baked cookies are preferred in our household. Cool for a few minutes before removing from pan.

This recipe can be doubled and cookies can all be baked and part of them frozen for later use ……..or save part of the dough and bake at a later time. I place a piece of waxed paper on the counter a make a long roll of dough, wrap it up in the paper and double wrap with plastic wrap or foil. When I want to bake more, I can just unwrap and slice off pieces and bake the slices.

CHRISTMAS COOKIES

    When I was little, one of the big events of Christmas was going to my Grandma Bearman's house and making Christmas cookies. My mom and usually Aunt Mildred were there along with my little brothers and cousins. It would be a long evening and the big kitchen table would be full of rolled out cookie dough for us to use the cookie cutters on, to make tons of cookies. The grownups would talk, we kids would listen to the radio, chase each other around and get in the way of the adults. Sometimes we had Christmas Carolers from our church come and sing carols out in the snowy yard. They all got some of our cookies and something warm to drink. The most fun was frosting and putting on the colored sugar. We made some beautiful cookies.

    I tried to repeat this joy with my daughters and grandchildren. I know our daughters have also done it with the grandchildren. When we made it in our kitchen, much smaller than in Grandma's huge farm kitchen, it didn't matter that the youngest was still in the high chair and the others on stools or standing on chairs to reach the kitchen table, we all had a grand messy time. Each time it brought back those wonderful memories of being so excited about Christmas and making cookies.

    Our Christmas was nothing like the ones of today. There were very few presents, Santa's load was much lighter then. We received more gifts than our parents and our Grandparents were happy to get an orange or anything. We had all the excitement of the Christmas tree and my Grandma always had a village around their tree. The tree was in the parlor and that had large double doors that were closed except for special occasions, Christmas being one of those. We always had the family gathering at Grandma's house. We drew names for gifts and it was such a big secret. We just couldn't wait to find out who had our name. Plus, we got the extra present.

Christmas Time

SOUR CREAM SUGAR COOKIES

3 Cups all purpose flour
1 ¼ tsp baking powder
½ tsp baking soda
1/8 tsp salt

1 ½ cups granulated sugar
½ butter or margarine
   at room temperature
1 cup low fat sour cream
1 egg
2 tsp vanilla

1. In a medium size bowl combine flour, baking powder, baking soda and salt. In a large bowl cream the granulated sugar and butter with electric mixer on medium speed,, until fluffy. Scrape sides of pan often.
2. Add the sour cream, egg, and vanilla, beating well. Use a wooden spoon and stir in flour mixture just until flour disappears. Divide the dough into 3 equal parts. Wrap each piece of dough in plastic wrap and refrigerate for one hour or until thoroughly chilled and easy to handle.
3. Preheat oven to 375 degrees. On a lightly flour surface, roll out 1 piece of dough to ¼ inch thickness and cut into shapes with cookie cutters. With spatula, transfer the cookies to un-greased cookie sheets, placing them about 2 "apart. Bake 8 to 10 minutes or until edges are firm and bottoms are lightly browned. Remove from oven and cool on wire racks. Repeat with rest of dough.

FROSTING
4. 2 cups   powdered sugar   ½ tsp. vanilla   3 Tbsp low fat milk
    (You may add food coloring if you wish.)
 To prepare the frosting, in a medium size bowl stir together the powdered sugar and ½ the milk plus the vanilla. Gradually stir in the remaining milk to reach the right consistency to spread on the cookies as frosting. You may need to make additional frosting.

This is not my Grandma's recipe but it is very similar.

Grandma and Grandpa Bearman

PEANUT BUTTER COOKIES

2 ½ cups flour	1 cup margarine or butter
½ tsp soda	1 cup granulated sugar
1 tsp baking powder	1 cup packed brown sugar
2 eggs	2 tsp vanilla
1 cup peanut butter	

Sift flour and measure, resift 3 times with soda and baking powder.
Mix sugars together, add eggs, margarine, peanut butter and mix very well. Add flour mixture and mix until forms dough. Knead in bowl only long enough to form a smooth dough.
Divide into 4 parts and form each part into a roll about 1" in diameter. Cut into 1" length pieces. Roll pieces in palm to form a small ball. Lay on un-greased cookie sheet about 1" apart. Press with fork tines to form crisscrosses. Bake 10 min at 375 degrees.
Makes about 7 doz. cookies.

SUGAR COOKIES

2 cups white sugar	2 tsp. Baking powder
1 cup Crisco	1 tsp soda
3 eggs	pinch of salt
3 ½ cups all purpose flour	1 cup sour milk

Cream sugar and Crisco. Add beaten eggs and sour milk. Add dry ingredients and beat well. (To make sour milk add 1 Tbsp vinegar to 1 cup minus 1 Tbsp of sweet milk) Drop on floured cookie sheet by spoonful. Press flat with back of spoon, sprinkle sugar on top. Bake 6 minutes at 450 Degrees.

This recipe comes from Nancy Springer, my sister-in-law and good friend. She is another great cook and has many delicious recipes.

CRISSCROSSED PEANUT BUTTER COOKIES

This is very similar to the other Cookie but easier. This was given to me by Lisa (our 3rd daughter and another terrific cook)

1 cup shortening (margarine or butter)
1 cup granulated sugar
1 cup packed brown sugar
3 cups sifted all purpose flour
2 tsp baking soda
2 eggs
1 tsp vanilla
1 cup peanut butter
½ tsp salt

Thoroughly cream shortening, sugar, eggs and vanilla. Stir in peanut butter. Sift in dry ingredients, stir into creamed mixture. Drop by rounded teaspoons on un-greased cookie sheet. Press with back of floured fork to make crisscrosses. Bake at 350degrees about 10 minutes. Makes approx. 5 dozen. Cookies.

OATMEAL COOKIES

1 cup margarine or butter
1 cup packed brown sugar
½ cup white sugar
2 eggs
1 tsp vanilla
1 cup raisins
1 ½ cup all purpose flour
1 tsp baking soda
1 tsp cinnamon
¼ tsp salt
3 cups Oatmeal (regular or quick)
1 cup nuts

Beat Margarine and sugars together till creamy, add eggs and vanilla. Beat well.
Add flour, cinnamon, soda & salt. Mix well
Stir in oats, raisins and nuts. Drop rounded Tbsp on un-greased cookie sheet.
Bake for 8- 10 min. in preheated 350 degree oven.
Cool for 1 or 2 minutes before removing from pan.

Marlo Ann

My Aunt Sally is very special to me, she is ten years older than I am and was always more like a big sister than my aunt. In looking back, she stood by me with more patience than if she had been a sister. She is my mom's youngest sister and I see some of her wonderful traits have been passed down to my daughters. We kids would always love to go to Aunt Sally and Uncle Dewey's. They were lots of fun to be with. I baby sat for my cousins and went with them on vacations. That is where the wander bug got me, as I love to travel to new places. Aunt Sally I thank you for all you have done for me and will never forget your patience and understanding. Aunt Sally always made cookies and her other two specialties were potato soup and the best macaroni & cheese ever. Here are two of her cookie recipes

PINEAPPLE COOKIES

1 cup brown sugar   2 eggs
1 cup white sugar   1 cup crushed pineapple
1 cup shortening (margarine or butter)   (well drained)
Sift together and then add
4 cups flour (or can substitute 1 ½ flour & 3 cups oatmeal)
2 tsp baking powder   ¼ tsp salt
1 tsp baking soda   ½ cup chopped nuts

Mix together, chill dough. Drop by Tbsp on greased cookie sheet. Bake 8-9 minutes .in a 350 degree pre heated oven. Be sure oven is preheated. These are crispy cookies. These can also be put in rolls, placed on waxed paper, chilled and sliced off, & baked. This is the easiest way to make the cookies. I have had best results because they are very chilled.

COCOANUT COOKIES

The above recipe except substitute for pineapple, ½ cup cocoanut
Instead of 4 cups flour use 1 ½ cup flour and 3 cups oatmeal
Use only 1 tsp baking soda (no baking powder)

Candy

We all love a good piece of fudge. I have made fudge since a little kid. On many a cold winter evening my big brother, Gene, would ask me to make some fudge. Of course everyone agreed that was a great idea. So we would have fudge and get out the popcorn popper and have popcorn with it. Whenever Ron would get sick, he would ask for some fudge. I could never understand that, but it made him feel better. Now our daughters usually make the fudge for the holidays but I still dig out the old recipes and make it when the mood strikes.

My favorite homemade candy was brown sugar candy or Penoche. After I was married and moved to California, my mom would make it for me and send it with our Christmas box. She made the best there ever was. The last batch she sent me I kept in the freezer for years and years, as I knew her hands had prepared it and it was comforting to keep part of her with me. When we moved from Southern California to Northern California and sold our house etc. I parted with my last brown sugar candy, made by my mom.

Here is her recipe for **PENOCHE**
2 cups brown sugar   2 Tbsp butter
½ cup cream   1/3 cup chopped nuts

Combine sugar, cream and butter. Boil to a soft boil stage
(234 - 238 deg. F) Remove from heat. Cool to room temperature. Beat till creamy, add nuts, continue beating until mixture will hold it's shape. Pour into well buttered shallow pan. Cut in squares.

HERSHEY FUDGE
2/3 cup Hershey cocoa   4 Tbsp butter
3 cups sugar   1 tsp vanilla
1/8 tsp salt   ½ cup chopped nuts (if desired)
1 ½ cup milk (I use skim or 1% or 2%)

Put all except butter and vanilla in large heavy sauce pan
(Large enough so candy will not boil over and heavy so it won't burn on the bottom, use a 3 or 4 qt pan). Stir together and bring to a boil, boil to med ball stage for soft fudge or hard ball stage if you like hard fudge. Boil on med heat approx 20 minutes, stir to keep from burning on the bottom and boiling over. (if you do not have a candy thermometer, take a cup with cold water and let a drop fall from your spoon into the water. The fudge will instantly harden and you can determine how hard it is.) When at the right ball stage, remove from heat, add vanilla and butter but do not stir. Let sit until cooled.. Beat with wooden spoon until it turns from shiny to dull in color. At this time you can add nuts if you wish. When it starts to set up it goes off fast, so have a well buttered plate ready. (If it is cold out, I often set it outside to cool down faster or set in a sink of cold water. Keep lid on pan).

MICROWAVE FUDGE
Our youngest daughter, Laurie, always made this one for us.

1 Lb. powdered sugar	½ cup cocoa
¼ cup milk	¼ cup butter
1 Tbsp vanilla	½ cup chopped nuts

Blend sugar and cocoa in bowl. Then add milk and butter. DO NOT MIX. Microwave for 2 minutes. Remove from oven, stir just to mix. Add vanilla and nuts, stir till blended. Pour into greased pan, cool in refrigerate for one hour before cutting and serving.

MICROWAVE PEANUT BRITTLE

1 cup raw peanuts	1 tsp butter or margarine
1 cup granulated sugar	1 tsp vanilla
½ cup light corn syrup	1 tsp baking soda
Dash of salt	

Stir together peanuts, corn , corn syrup and salt in a 1 ½ qt. Casserole or microwave safe glass mixing bowl

Place in microwave and cook 4 minutes, remove from oven, stir contents. Return to oven and cook 3 ½ minutes Add butter, vanilla and baking soda to syrup, stirring to blend well. Return to microwave and cook 1 minute, stir, then return to oven and cook ½ to 1 minute more. The syrup will be VERY HOT. The syrup mix should be a light brown. At the final time, you should check it at the ½ minute and if it is a nice light brown, you need not cook further. (If overcooked it will burn) I LEARNED FROM EXPERIENCE.

Pour onto a lightly buttered cookie sheet and let cool for half an hour or so before breaking into serving pieces. Store in an airtight container.

I have used salted peanuts, macadamia & cashew nuts.

On other recipes I have read, an additional ideas is to pour some chocolate chips over the
 top of the hot brittle and spread them as they melt. It sounds good but I have not tried it.

The prep time for this is about 5 minutes. But it needs your undivided attention. So put aside about 15 minutes to make. The time does not include the cooling time nor the eating time.

This makes a pound of candy.

I also had better results when the weather was not raining. The humidity seems to affect how brittle it gets. This is my own personal observation.

DIVINITY

(Read all the directions first as some preparations need to be made in order. Also, needs undivided attention and need to work fast.)

1st. Beat 3 egg whites (in a large glass mixing bowl) as dry as possible . Set aside.

2nd In a 3 quart sauce pan put
    3 cups granulated sugar
    ½ cup corn syrup
    ½ cup hot water

Boil the sugar, corn syrup and water for approx. 4 minutes on medium heat. Stir constantly so it doesn't burn.

Should be hard ball stage, on candy thermometer 255 degree .f (If no thermometer put drop of syrup drop in cold water and should make a tinkle sound on side of cup or glass.)

3rd Pour ½ hot cooked syrup in a thin thread into the egg whites, beating with mixer on low, constantly. Then put rest of syrup on stove to get bubbling hot again and pour rest into egg whites, the same way, mixing constantly.

4th instantly add 1 tsp vanilla
        1 cup nuts (chopped very fine) Stir in well

5th Have a large piece of foil on the counter and spoon the divinity   with a teaspoon out onto the foil, Use a table knife to help get off spoon. If divinity gets too stiff, add 1 teaspoon of boiling water and stir in well. Continue to drop onto foil.

Peanut Brittle

FRUITY CANDY

This is a recipe from Ron's Mother, Lily Anne Wasson. She loved fruit filled candy.

½ cup Honey   ½ cup peanut butter
½ cup cocoa or Carob powder ½ cup raisins or dates
2 cups, total mixture of   ½ cup shredded cocoanut
Sesame seeds, Sunflower seeds and chopped nuts

Heat honey and peanut butter in a middle size sauce pan. Quickly add cocoa or carob. Stir. Remove from heat. Add seeds, nuts and cocoanut and dried fruit. Pour into a greased 8" square pan and refrigerate to harden. Cut into squares. Keep in the refrigerator,

CHEWY SESAME CANDY   no cooking
This recipe is from a friend, Sonya.

1 cup raw honey   1 cup natural peanut butter
1 cup carob powder   1 cup sunflower seeds
1 cup sesame seeds.

Mix ingredients with a mixer. Spread in 8" square pan, cut into squares or make balls and roll in cocoanut. Freeze. Take them out a few minutes before serving.

RICE CRISPY CANDY   (microwave)
¼ Cup butter   4 cups miniature marshmallows
5 cups rice crispy cereal

Melt butter in 3 qt casserole and add marshmallows, cook in the microwave until marshmallows are melted and mixture is syrup. (stir every 30 seconds) Remove from microwave and add rice crispy cereal. Stir till well coated. Press firmly in buttered 13 X 9" pan.

RICE CRISPIES MARSHMALLOW SQUARES

¼ cup butter or margarine   1 tsp. vanilla
½ pound marshmallows   1 package Rice Crispy cereal
   (30 large marshmallows)   (5 ½ oz)

Cook butter and marshmallows over medium heat until syrupy. Add vanilla and beat toughly. Put Rice Crispy cereal in buttered large bowl and pour marshmallow mixture on top, stirring briskly. Press into buttered 9x13" pan. Cut into squares when cooled.

FANTASY FUDGE

Preparation time 10 min. Cooking time 15 min.

3 cups sugar
¾ cup butter (1 ½ sticks)
1 small can (5 oz.) Evaporated milk or (2/3 cup)
2 squares Bakers semi-sweet chocolate, chopped up
1 (7 oz.) Jar Marshmallow cream
1 tsp vanilla   1 cup chopped nuts

Heat sugar, butter & evaporated milk to full rolling boil in a heavy 3 quart saucepan. Stir on medium heat until candy thermometer registers 234 degrees, about 4 minutes, stirring constantly. If no thermometer, cook 4 minutes and it will be between a hard and soft ball stage. Remove from heat.
2. Stir in chocolate and marshmallow, stir till melted. Then add Vanilla and nuts, stir together.
3. Spread immediately in foil lined or well buttered 9" square pan. Cool at room temperature at least 4 hours.

SEE'S FUDGE

I have collected two of this recipe over the years and it has been many years, considering the ancient old paper they are on.

4 ½ cup sugar   3 (6 oz.) packages chocolate chips
1 large can evaporated milk   1 jar Marshmallow cream
1 stick (¼ lb) butter   1 tsp vanilla
4 cups nuts chopped

Combine sugar and milk, bring to a boil and boil on low for
12 minutes. Pour boiled mixture over remaining ingredients
(Except nuts) and beat until thick. Stir in nuts and pour into buttered pan. Let stand overnight in the refrigerator. Cut into squares.

Why I mention the age of the above recipe is because the year, 2005, I cut out of a magazine The Brigittine Monks Fudge recipe. It is almost exactly the same as the See's Fudge. The difference is:
 2 sticks of butter instead of one
 2 cups of nuts instead of 4
 Cook exactly 6 minutes instead of 12

Marlo Ann

Cakes

Family gatherings were a normal thing for our family. We lived in Southern California, our daughters grew up there and then we had the weddings and the babies, the grandchildren,   There were many family gatherings. We were constantly making the various cakes and deserts etc. for birthdays, showers, holidays and just being together. Now the families have spread out, living up and down the Western Coast and Grandchildren are not little any longer. Life changes and we all move on.   Thank goodness for all the happy memories of the good family times we have had together and look forward to the ones ahead of us.

Fruit Cocktail Cake

Wild Roses and Childhood Memories

This cake recipe was given to my by daughter, Debbie. It is one she used to make for various occasions.

FRUIT COCKTAIL CAKE

1 White Cake Mix
1 16oz can fruit cocktail (Very Well drained)
Use whole eggs instead of whites only and add the drained fruit cocktail. Follow directions on box and bake as normal.
Frost with the following Butter Cream frosting and sprinkle with cocoanut.

BUTTER CREAM FROSTING
¼ cup butter   2 cups powdered sugar
1 tsp. Vanilla   2 tablespoon milk

Cream butter well and slowly add the sugar, mixing well. Add vanilla and slowly mix in the milk. If too thick to spread add a little more milk and if too thin, add a little more sugar, Mix very well , spread on cooled cake. Sprinkle on cocoanut before frosting sets.

CARROT CAKE

3 cups grated carrots (set aside)   2 cups sugar
1 ½ cup oil   4 eggs
2 tsp. Vanilla   2 cups flour
2 tsp soda   1 tsp. salt
2 tsp baking powder   2 tsp. cinnamon
                                     2/3 cup chopped nuts

Mix sugar, flour, soda, baking powder together, then add eggs and beat well. Stir in the remaining ingredients and mix well.
Pour into three cake pans for traditional three layer carrot cake.
Or pour into 13 ½ x 9" sheet cake pan

Frost with Cream Cheese frosting

1 stick margarine or butter   1 lb. Powdered sugar
1 (8 oz) package cream cheese   1 tsp. vanilla

Have butter and cream cheese room temp. Cream all ingredients together and spread over layers and top of cake if making layers, Or on top of the sheet cake.

The first time I ever had carrot cake was the year an extended family member (Brother John) brought us a huge bag of carrots. The girls were all in the teenage bracket and ate lots of veggies, but I tried to figure out how to use the carrots. Lisa found the Carrot Cake recipe, and we made our first one of many.

WINE CAKE

Kathy is the famous wine cake baker. This has been her specialty for years. She always made it for us at Christmas & Holiday times, It is delicious.

1 package of yellow Cake mix (not a butter cake)
1 small package Vanilla instant pudding
¾ cup oil
1 tsp. Nutmeg
¾ cup of Cream of Sherry
4 eggs.
Mix ingredients above together for 5 minutes,
Bake 1 hour at 350 degrees in bunt pan. Sprinkle top with
 powdered sugar after removing cake from pan, while still warm.

The following cake recipe is from our youngest daughter, Laurie. She usually had more fun things to do than cook, but she can do anything she sets her mind too, including cooking.

LAURIE'S APPLESAUCE CAKE

1/3 cup sugar   1 Tbsp cinnamon (mix in bowl, set aside)
1 yellow cake mix   3 eggs   1 16 oz can applesauce
In a greased 9X13" sheet cake pan, dust with 1 tbsp of sugar and cinnamon mix. Set aside.   Blend cake mix, applesauce & eggs. Beat 4 minutes, medium speed, pour half into cake pan, spread evenly. Sprinkle with half sugar and cinnamon mix , pour in rest of cake mix, spread and sprinkle with remaining sugar & cinnamon.
Bake at 350 degrees for 40 minutes.
For variety can sprinkle nuts, cocoanut or raisins on first layer.
Can be frosted with White Butter frosting if desired.

Wild Roses and Childhood Memories

My Mom made a wonderful Black Walnut cake and my Aunt May made a wonderful Hickory Nut cake. I had my Mom's recipe for years and when asking relatives for some of these old favorites, I obtained it from my Aunt May. Well, I have discovered they are the same basic cake recipe; the different nuts make the different flavors.

When these cakes were going to be baked it would be for special occasions, as it was a lot of effort. First thing, one of the kids had to go out and crack the nuts and take the meat out of the shells, with a nut pick. Most young cooks today don't realize how much work that is. To back track, in the fall we had to go out and gather the nuts from the trees after they fell. They have a green outer husk and black inner covering on them that has to be removed. This task made our hands black, especially the black walnut. We didn't have gloves, so had black hands for a few days. The nuts would be dried and stored. When we were told by our Mothers that they needed some nuts for a cake, we knew the morning was shot. The hard shells are very hard to crack. We had a small piece of old railroad track rail approximately 6" to a foot long. Put a nut on the piece of track and hit it with a hammer. You didn't hit it too hard as the meat inside would all be smashed, sometimes it was your finger. You soon learned the knack.

The meat inside these nuts are not nearly as large as what we usually use now, English Walnuts. They are a joy to crack and take the meat out. It would take us hours to get enough nutmeats for a cake. We then had to check and double check to be sure there were no shell among them. If you bit down on a piece of hickory or black walnut shell, good-by tooth. The redeeming factor was our mouths watering for the delicious cake that would be forthcoming.

I have a jar of some nutmeats that my younger brother, Ken, had picked out for me. He had cancer and couldn't do much to fill his time. On a visit to see him, he and I sat together and filled a jar with nutmeats. I see them in my freezer and remember the time together and lots of memories we had growing up. We were close.

Marlo Ann and little brother Kenny

The basic cake recipe for **BLACK WALNUT OR HICKORY NUT**

Cream: 1 ¼ cups shortening
        1 tsp almond extract and 1 tsp vanilla
Add: 1 ½ cups sugar
        4 egg yolk
        Mix together until fluffy
Add: 3 ½ cups sifted cake flour
        5 tsp baking powder
        1 tsp salt
Alternately with
        1 ½ cups milk
Add ¼ cup sugar to 4 egg whites and beat until glossy
Add 1 ½ cup nuts, Hickory for Hickory Nut cake or
        Black Walnut for Black Walnut cake
Pour egg whites and nuts into other ingredients. Fold in batter.

Pour into 9x13" greased & floured baking pan, Bake 350 degrees for 45 minutes. Or pour into 2 8" layer cake pans and bake 25 to 30 minutes Check with the tooth pick method.

Frost with Whipped Cream or a Butter Cream frosting when cooled. Can sprinkle a few nuts on top.

First four generations (women) of our family

SAUERKRAUT CAKE

I know everyone is surprised at how delicious this cake is. I have not introduced it as sauerkraut cake because the first reaction is, how can you make a cake with kraut? Well you can.

2/3 cup butter or margarine	2 ¼ cup sifted flour
1 ½ cup sugar	1 tsp baking soda
3 eggs	1 tsp baking powder
1 tsp vanilla	¼ tsp salt
½ cup cocoa	cup water
	2/3 cup rinsed, drained and Chopped sauerkraut

Cream the butter with sugar. Beat in eggs, one at a time. Add vanilla,
Sift together cocoa, flour, baking powder, soda and salt. Add to creamed mixture alternately with water. Stir in the kraut.
Pour into 2 greased and floured 8" baking pan. Bake at 350 degrees, 30 minutes or until cake tests done. Or can bake in 9 x 13" cake pan for approx. 45 minutes, test for doneness.
(the sauerkraut has the texture of cocoanut)

Can frost with whipped cream, Mocha Cream or Cool Whip per serving. A Chocolate frosting can be used.

Mocha Cream

Whip 1 ½ cups heavy whipping cream with 3 tbsp sugar, 1 tbsp instant coffee, 2 tsp cocoa and 1 tsp rum (optional) until soft peaks form.

Marlo Ann

ITALIAN CREAM CAKE

This recipe comes from Nancy Springer, but she obtained it from our Sister-in law, Marlene Springer. It is one of her family favorites.

1. Separate 5 eggs. They should be room temp. Put the whites in a medium size glass or ceramic mixing bowl. Beat egg whites until stiff and dry. Put in refrigerator

2. Cream together
    1 cup Crisco and 2 cups sugar
    Add the 5 large egg yolks One at a time.

3. 1 cup buttermilk   2 cups flour (sifted)
   1 tsp vanilla   1 tsp soda
   1 cup cocoanut   1 tsp baking powder
   1 cup chopped nuts   5 egg whites (beaten)

Add flour sifted, with baking soda &, baking powder, alternating with buttermilk. Add vanilla, cocoanut and pecans. Mix. Quickly fold in egg whites. Bake at 350 degrees or 25 to 30 minutes in three 9 " layer cake pans. (or 8" pans) check for doneness.

Frosting

1 8 oz cream cheese   1 tsp. Vanilla
½ stick butter or margarine   1 cup cocoanut
1 lb. Box powdered sugar   1 cup chopped nuts

Cream together cream cheese and butter. Add the rest of ingredients one at a time, mix. Spread between each layer and top and sides.

FRUIT CAKE

My Mom made a wonderful fruit cake, The Ladies Aid at our Lutheran Church used her recipe and her help in making these to sell as fund raisers. They would sell all they could make. I have used her recipe for years and have made various experiments and changes etc. with the recipe. Here is the basic recipe and it is very responsive to adding more fruit or nuts of different kinds.

1/3 cup shortening	1 cup white raisins
1 egg	1 cup chopped dates
1 tsp. Soda	4 cups nuts chopped
1 tsp. Baking powder	1 cup figs chopped
1 tsp cinnamon	1 cup dried apricots
½ tsp nutmeg	2 cups candied fruit
½ tsp cloves	1 cup brown sugar
½ tsp salt	1 cup warm applesauce
1 ½ cup flour	1 cup glazed cherries

Cream shortening and sugar, add beaten egg.
Sift all dry ingredients and add with applesauce, alternately to the creamed shortening and sugar. Add all fruits and nuts, Mix well.

Grease loaf pans with oil, then cut brown paper or parchment paper to fit bottoms and side and line pans and grease again with oil. Bake in slow oven at 300 to 325 degrees about 1 ½ hour. Recipe will make several loaves. Remove and turn over from pan when slightly cooled to a cake rack.

Glaze for cooled Fruit Cake
½ cup white corn syrup, ½ cup orange juice mix together. Boil for 2 or 3 minutes, do very little stirring. While hot, brush on top of cake. Place ½ candied cherries & nuts on top and brush on glaze.

Fruit Cake

Marlo Ann

Many a cool evening, when we were outside playing we would come into the house and Mom would have a cake waiting for us. Our appetites were always good. I can visualize us and smell the aroma of that cake coming out of the old wood cook stove oven.

Mom's CHOCOLATE RED DEVILS FOOD CAKE

1. Cream together
    - ½ cup shortening
    - 1 cup sugar
2. 1 egg, add & beat together
3. 1 cup boiling water
    - ½ cup cocoa
   Stir cocoa and water till smooth
   And add to above
4. 1 cup sour milk
    - 1 ¼ tsp baking soda
    - (mix together)
5. 2 ½ cups cake flour
    - 1 ½ tsp baking powder
    - ½ tsp salt
    - 2 tsp vanilla
6. Alternately add #4 & 5 to mixture of 1-2-.3 Mix very well & bake in a greased & floured 7 ½ x 11" pan 350 degrees 35 to 40 min. Check for doneness. Can bake in 2 round 8 in. pans, 25 to 30 min.

This cake is quite similar and it was my Grandma Springer's

DEVIL'S FOOD CAKE

Cream together
2 cups sugar
½ cup shortening
Add 2 eggs (beat together well)
½ cup cocoa dissolved in ½ cup
Boiling water, beat till smooth, add
To above mixture   Beat well

Add 1 cup sweet milk
1 tsp vanilla Beat well
Sift 2 cups flour and
1 tsp soda together 3 times.
Add to cake mixture and
Beat all together well.

Pour into two round greased & floured 8 in. pans for 25 to 30 min. Or a 7 ½ X 11"pan for 35 to 40 min. check for doneness.

Frostings

BASIC BUTTER CREAM FROSTING

¼ Cups butter or margarine
2 Cups powdered sugar
1 Tsp vanilla
2 Tbsp milk
Cream butter well, slowly add sugar, vanilla, work in and add milk until smooth and easy spreading consistency. If too thin add more sugar and too thick, add more milk. Beat well.

To make chocolate, add either 2 sq. melted chocolate or
1/3 cup cocoa in 1 Tbsp hot water (or hot coffee for Mocha)
Beat well.

Marlo Ann - 52 -

"NO COOK" MARSHMALLOW FROSTING

¼ tsp salt   ¾ Corn Syrup (Karo)
2 egg whites   1 ¼ tsp vanilla
¼ cup sugar

Add salt to egg white and beat till it forms soft peaks. Gradually add sugar, beating until smooth and glossy. Slowly add Karo syrup, beating thoroughly after each addition until firmly peaked. Fold in vanilla. Spread on cooled cake.

MARSHMALLOW ICING

Combine in a double boiler
2 egg whites unbeaten
1 ½ cup sugar
6 Tbsp. water
6 quartered marshmallows

Mix together just to blend. Place over boiling water and cook, beating constantly with beater until it peaks (about 5 minutes) Remove from heat.
Add ¼ tsp cream of tartar
1 tsp. vanilla. Beat till stiff

SATINY ICING

Combine in saucepan and stir well
½ cup firmly packed light brown sugar
¼ cup corn syrup
2 Tbsp. water

Bring slowly to boil, cook to 240 degrees or till forms a soft ball in cold water. Meanwhile or in advance: Beat ½ cup of egg whites till stiff but not dry. Use large mixing bowl.
Gradually pour hot liquid in a thin stream into the egg whites beating constantly, continue beating until spreading consistency. Blend in 1 tsp, vanilla. Frost cake.

PINEAPPLE CHEESECAKE

2 large or 4 small pkgs Philadelphia cream cheese
2 eggs unbeaten
½ cup sugar
1 small can crushed pinapple (well drained)
1 tsp vanilla   dash of cinnamon
1 graham cracker crust

Mix above ingredients together and place into graham cracker crust. Bake for 20 min. at 350 degree oven. Remove from oven and allow to cool for 1 hour. (DO NOT Refrigerate)When cool

Take ½ pint, (one 8 oz cup) sour cream, 3 Tbsp sugar & 1 tsp.vanilla. Mix together. Spread on cheese cake mixture. Refrigerate until serving.

CHERRY CHEESE CAKE

Our daughter, Laurie, is the champion Cherry Cheese cake maker.

1 pkg (8 oz) cream cheese
1 can Eagle Brand Sweetened condensed milk
½ cup Real Lemon lemon juice
1 1/2 tsp vanilla
1 can (1 lb.5oz.) cherry pie filling, chilled
1 graham cracker pie crust

Beat cream cheese until smooth. Gradually mix in sweetened condensed milk. Stir in lemon juice and vanilla. Spread in crust. Refrigerate 3-4 hours or till firm.

Top with cherry pie filling. Keep refrigerated until ready to serve.
Serves 8

Marlo Ann

Desserts

Four girls flying back to Indiana for the summer

Dear Debbie and all the rest of the Family. I hope everyone is O.K. we are all fine now. I had a rash on my hands. I had to wear gloves all the time. I should of had you here to wash my dishes & cloth and a bunch of other things I can't do with gloves on, It is better now, still itches a lot. I have to take medicine and put some on my hands yet.

Well I hope you all had a nice Easter. The bunnie was here to. the kids had a xercus. I got 3 plants and a coursange. 1 lilly, 1 tigerange and 1 azzalia and orchid coursage.

Well Debbie I hope you dedn't hold your breath waiting on that tapayoka recipt. I am sorry but did you ever try to write with gloves on (over) here it is.

½ lb bag tapayoka (Pearl)
8 cups water.
let soak over nite.
then cook over low heat till clear. take off
add ½ cup sugar.
1 lb marshmellows
½ teaspoon salt. and stir ocationely till marshmellow are dessolved.
then add 1-No 2½ can crushed pineapple (about 19¢)
1 cup chopped nuts.
1 cup wiffing cream. If pudding is thick add it cream just as is - if it is thin whip cream & add after pudding is cool. you may use more cream if desired

Debbie I doubt if you can find through this with Grandmas poor spelling and awful hand writing but maybe Mommie will help you translate it. Hope you have good luck and it taists good, let me know how it turnes out. Thanks for writing and we all love you and all the rest too. good bye to all and love Grandma

A reply letter with Tapioca Recipe

This dessert was one of my Mom's specialties. She had a special green pan that she would cook her tapioca in. When we saw that pan come out, it was OH BOY!! Mom's making Tapioca pudding.

TAPIOCA PUDDING

½ lb bag of Pearl tapioca
8 cups of water   Let SOAK overnight

Cook the above soaked tapioca and water over low heat until tapioca pearls are clear, take off the stove d
 add ½ cup sugar   ½ tsp. salt
1 lb marshmallows
Stir together until marshmallows are dissolved. Then add
1 No. 2 ½ can (about 1 qt.) of crushed pineapple, do not drain.
1 cup chopped nuts
1 cup whipping cream…. If tapioca seems thick add the cream un-whipped. If the tapioca seems thin, then whip the cream and add to pudding. Let cool. Add more cream as desired. Keep refrigerated.

Mom's green pan was a heavy enameled pan. The fire had to be low as you didn't want to scorch the tapioca as it cooked, so it was a long time preparing, especially over a wood cook stove. This dessert completed makes lots, so we got to eat bowls of it for a couple days, to our delight, as Mom didn't make it very often,

Our daughters spent most of one summer with my parents on the farm and their Grandma made the tapioca for them. Debbie wrote and asked for the recipe.

Aunt Zella was a great cook… She always brought a dessert when they would come and visit.   She had an elegant flair on presentation.

ZELLA'S DESSERT
1 can pie cherries (NOT pie filling)   ½ cup cocoanut
1 cube margarine   ½ cup chopped pecans
1 box white cake mix
Pour cherries in a buttered 9 X 13" cake pan. Do not drain. Sprinkle one box white cake mix over the top. Place cocoanut and nut on top of cake mix. Bake 1 hr. in preheated 350 degree oven.

PINEAPPLE UPSIDE DOWN CAKE

This is good baked in a well seasoned black iron skillet, 8 or 9". A Corning ware or metal cake pan can be used. You must be able to put on top of stove burner.

12 Tbsp Butter	½ cup milk	1 ½ cups flour
1 cup brown sugar	1 egg	2 tsp Baking Powder
¼ cup Pineapple juice		½ tsp salt
5 whole Pineapple rings		½ cup white sugar

A few Maraschino cherries can be placed inside the Pineapple rings after cake turned over.

Preheat oven to 400 deg. F. Melt 4 Tbsp of the butter in the skillet or baking pan. Stir in the brown sugar, cook over low heat until sugar dissolves. Remove from heat and add Pineapple juice. Arrange rings in one layer in pan. Set aside. Melt remaining butter in small pan, remove from heat and stir in the milk and egg, beat well. Mix the flour, Baking Powder, salt and sugar together. Add to the milk mixture and beat until smooth. Pour over pineapple and bake about 35 minutes. Do the toothpick test to be sure it is done. Cool in pan 10 minutes, turn out on a plate, fruit side up.

Until I moved to California I had never had a Chocolate Éclair or Creampuff. My Mother-In-Law loved them and we would go to a local bakery for a treat. Years later, a neighbor gave me a recipe and I would make them myself.

CHOCOLATE ECLAIRS

	(Filling & Frosting)
1 cup water	1 pkg. Vanilla pudding mix
½ cup butter or margarine	3 oz. size
½ tsp. Salt	½ cup heavy cream to whip
1 cup all purpose flour	(can just use whipped cream)
4 eggs, unbeaten	2 cups chocolate chips

1. Heat over to 400 degrees. In a large saucepan, combine 1 cup water with butter and salt. Heat over medium heat until butter melts and water boils.
2. Then turn heat to very low, add flour all at one and beat vigorously with wooden spoon, until dough leaves sides of pan in a smooth ball.
3. Immediately remove pan from heat. Beat in eggs, one at a time. Beat until smooth after each egg is added, when all eggs are blended, beat dough until smooth and shiny. Use wooden spoon.
4. On an un-greased cookie sheet, drop dough about 2 inches apart. For éclairs make long and cream puffs round.
5. Bake 35 to 40 min. till brown. Cool on cake rack.
6. Make pudding according to package; only use 1 ½ cup milk. Place in refrigerator, cover with wax paper, cool
7. When pudding is cool, whip cream. Beat pudding until smooth, fold in whipped cream. Fill éclairs. (You can use just cream)
8. Melt chocolate, front éclairs and refrigerate. Delicious

APPLES

Apples are such a wonderful delicious fruit. They not only taste good but are good for us. Wild Apples have been growing and people have been eating them for many thousands of years,

I went to school in a little one room, 8 grade brick schoolhouse. It was next to my Grandma and Grandpa Bearman's farm house. Their apple orchard was near the road and there was a dip in the fence which we made climbing over the fence. Jonathan Apple is an early fall apple and it ripened about the time school started in September. The most wonderful apple in the world is one you can climb over a fence and up a tree to pick.. When we walked home from school, we made this emergency stop. Our pockets were loaded up with apples, to last until we got home,. Our sack lunches were well worn off by the time we were out of school. We had to take our recess and lunch hour outside on the playground unless the weather was extremely bad. In the winter it took us half our time to get our coats and boots on and off. We had another hole in the fence between my Grandparents field and school yard. We could climb through this hole so we could play on the pond that would freeze over. No one thought about liability or trespassing in those days, we knew we just had to behave ourselves and have fun. Back to fall days and apple trees…………..Every fall I look for Jonathan apples and have such happy memories of those juicy red apples. I have a tree planted in my yard. So far the squirrels have enjoyed my apples.

My husband, Ron, at age 5 or 6

We used to pick apples by the bushel and would wrap each in a piece of paper and they would go in a big barrel in the fruit cellar. In the winter we could have a fresh apple. By the end of winter they were getting pretty wrinkled and not so good. Mom would then bake something to use them up. The term about one rotten apple can spoil a barrel full, it is true. Believe me!

MOM'S APPLE DUMPLINS

Mix together
2 cups flour and 2 tsp Baking Powder
Cut in 2 Tbsp butter & 2 Tbsp shortening
½ tsp salt
Add 1 cup milk
Make a dough and roll out to approx ¼ inch thick
Cut ½ cube of butter into slices and place on dough
Peel and slice approx 1 quart or so of apples and place on the dough, in a row across the center,

Sprinkle 1 cup white sugar mixed with 1 tsp Cinnamon over the apples. Fold the edges up from the sides to cover apples,.
You now have one big roll of dough with the apples in the center.
Slice off in approx 1" slices and place slices side by side (can be crowded if necessary) in a greased 9X13" pan and bake at 350 degrees preheated oven for total of 25 to 30 minutes. After putting apples in the oven, make the following:
Bring to a boil in a small pan
    1 cup white sugar
    2 Tbsp flour
    1 cup water
    ¼ tsp cinnamon

After Apple Dumplins have baked 15 minutes, take out of oven & pour sauce over them, return to oven to finish baking 15 min.

Serve warm or cold with whipped cream or ice cream or cold milk.

Marlo Ann

APPLE RAISIN CRUNCH

4 medium apples (Granny Smith, Pippin)   ¾ cup Quaker Oats
1 cup golden raisins   1 tsp cinnamon
¼ cup orange juice   1 stick butter
1 cup + 2 Tbsp brown sugar   1 tsp grated orange zest
1 cup all purpose flour

1. Preheat oven to 400 degrees F. and grease a 2 qt. baking dish
2. Peel. Core and slice the apples into ¼" slices
3. In the baking dish, combine the apples with the raisins, orange juice, orange zest, 2 Tbsp of the sugar.
4. In a medium-sized bowl, mix the flour, remaining 1 cup sugar, oats and cinnamon. Cut in the butter with a pastry blender or two knives, until mixture is crumbly. Sprinkle on top of apples and raisins.
5. Bake for 30 minutes or till top is golden   This makes 8 servings.

For A really decadent crunch, or crisp or cobbler, drizzle a few tablespoon of melted butter before sticking in the oven.

Of course this will be delicious with some vanilla ice-cream or a dab of whipped cream on top.

JOHNNY APPLESEED

Being from Indiana, Johnny Appleseed was always a recognizable name. The proper name was John Chapman, born in Massachusetts in1774. He left his home early in life to follow the Pioneers, intending to teach the Bible and plant Apple seeds and cuttings.. He dedicated his life to this mission and died in Indiana in 1854, at one of his apple orchards.

I have planted a Heritage Johnny Appleseed apple tree in my yard. So far have not had a crop of apples but it is a young tree.

APPLE CRISP

3 To 5 Apples peeled and sliced
¾ cups Quaker Oats (preferred Quick cooking)
¾ cup brown sugar
½ cup flour
½ cup butter or margarine

Mix oats, sugar, flour, add butter and mix with fork. Mixture will be crumbly. Place apples in a lightly greased 8" square baking pan. Pour the dough mixture over apples.
Bake approx 35 minutes at 350 degree oven. Serves 6
Serve with vanilla ice- cream, whipped cream or cool whip

In the spring, the first apples that came ripe were a tender green apple. They were great to eat but better for cooking and making pies or baking. Mom would make lots of baked apples.

BAKED APPLES

6 apples, cut in half and cored
Place upright in baking dish
Sprinkle 1 Tbsp sugar on each half (more or less depends on tartness of apple)
Add 3 or 4 Candied Red Hot candies to each half.
Put in oven and bake approx 20 to 25 minutes, 350 degree oven. Check for doneness at 20 minutes. When apples are tender, remove from oven, Place a Marshmallow on each half and put back in oven until marshmallow has melted and is slightly browned.
Serve while warm. If apples are not very juicy, add a small amount of water to baking dish. Any juice can be served with the apple. It's an easy side dish to serve with ham or pork main dishes, or just to enjoy as a baked apple.

One room schoolhouse

Pies

Pies are my personal favorite dessert, especially fruit pies. I have a fond memory of a day with my mom and Chocolate Pie.

As I had written earlier, my Mom had more work to do than an army, so she didn't have time to play. Our time together was working together. One day she took us for a picnic out in our woods. As little kids, we loved to go out there, part of it was cleared so we could run and play, pick wild flowers, morel mushrooms and pretend we were pioneers. Sometimes we wandered into the uncleared areas and pretended we were Explorers. We wondered if the mounds of dirt we found under big trees were Indian burial grounds. We were looking for arrowheads. Many times a neighbor would come over and tell Mom they saw us out in those wood and we got a scolding and told of all the dangers out there. This day was really special because Mom was with us and we could all pick wild flowers and have a chocolate pie for our picnic. That was the best Chocolate Pie I ever had and more ironic, Chocolate Pie is my husbands favorite pie. She must have known.

We had fences to separate the fields and wild roses grew along them. They smelled so good and looked so pretty. The farms do not have the fences like years ago and the field rows are mostly gone. So are the wild roses. There are the memories of a little girl, barefoot, running in the earth, through the fields. Bringing home a handful of wild flowers, picked for her Mom.

Wild Flowers in my Yard

MOM"S CREAM PIE FILLINGS

Basic filling:
Mix in sauce pan 2/3 cup sugar   2 ½ tsp cornstarch
                  ½ tsp salt   1 Tbsp flour

Stir in gradually: 3 cups milk
Cook over medium heat, stir constantly till boils 1 minute. Remove from heat. Take at least 1 cup of hot mixture and blend SLOWLY with 3 slightly beaten egg yolks. Pour slowly back in the hot mixture, stirring constantly. Blend well and boil 1 minute more, stirring constantly.
Remove from heat and blend in 1 Tbsp butter and 1 ½ tsp vanilla. Cool, stir occasionally. Pour into cooled baked pie shell.

Variations: The above is Vanilla Cream

Banana Cream: Layer bottom of baked pie crust with sliced
               Bananas. Pour in filling and garnish with
               Whipped cream & bananas. Or make meringue

Chocolate Cream: Increase sugar in Basic Filling ingredients to
                  1 ½ cup. Add 3 squares cut up unsweetened
                  Chocolate with the milk addition. It will melt.
                  Mix in well. Follow Basic directions.
                  Whipped cream for the topping or meringue

Cocoanut Cream: Fold in ¾ cup moist shredded cocoanut into
                 Basic Filling just before pouring into baked , cooled
                 Pie crust shell. Sprinkle cocoanut over Whipped
                 Cream topping or make meringue.

LEMON PIE

1/3 cup corn starch
1/¼ cup sugar
¼ tsp salt
1 ½ cup boiling water

3 eggs separated
1/3 cup strained lemon juice
2 Tbsp butter
½ tsp graded lemon zest

1 baked 8" piecrust shell, cooled
6 Tbsp sugar

Mix corn starch, sugar, & salt in top of double boiler or heavy sauce pan. Stirring constantly, slowly add boiling water, Blend very well. Cook, stirring constantly until mixture is thick and clear. Set off stove. Beat egg yolks and stir a little of the hot mixture in egg yolks, stirring constantly. Pour slowly back into the pan of hot mixture, stirring constantly. Put back on stove and cook 2 more minutes, continue stirring. Remove from stove, add lemon juice, butter and lemon zest. Mix well. Cool and pour into cooled, baked pie shell.

Beat the egg whites until barely stiff and add the 6 Tbsp sugar gradually and again beat till stiff. Swirl over pie filling, to touch the edge of the crust all around. Place in preheated 350 deg. Oven until egg whites (meringue) are a golden brown about 10 min.
Cool before cutting.

Be sure when you when squeezing lemons for pie that you strain all the seeds out. I made the error of being in a hurry and made the most beautiful lemon pie but had left a seed in. The seed made it a horrible bitter tasting pie.

MINCEMEAT

Many people don't even know what mincemeat is today, but it was a very popular way of preserving meats without salting or smoking it. Traditionally, the meat, along with suet, was combined with fruits, spices and some spirits, (liquor) packed in jars and sealed with wax. At Holiday time it was wonderful to have for festive pies. It would be made well ahead of the Holiday Season and it would keep indefinitely, and mellowed out by the time for winter festivities.

I have never cared for the meat mincemeat, but my mom made a Mock Mincemeat, using green tomatoes instead of meat. We had Mincemeat pies for Thanksgiving and Christmas, as well as Mincemeat bars. Mom provided me with some jars of her Mincemeat and I would make at least one pie at the Holidays. My father-in-law grew up in Ohio, and he could appreciate the tradition. When I had used up my last jar I lamented to our eldest daughter, Debbie, who also like the mincemeat pie, that it was gone. The store purchased product just did not taste as good as the home made.
For Christmas, Debbie gave me the greatest gift. She had written my relatives to see if she could locate the recipe my Mom had used to make her Mincemeat. My Aunt sent it to her, and she prepared a batch of it, canned it in glass jars and gave it to me. What thought went into the gift and it meant so very much.

To add some additional comments to the above story, Debbie had to find and buy the green tomatoes. Transport all these ingredients to her cabin, which is out in the high desert of Southern California. She has no city water but has to go a mile or so and get water in a tank and bring back to the cabin. A reminiscence of how much more difficult the tasks are when there are no modern conveniences.

Desert Riders
and
Our Cabin in the Desert

(Which now belongs to Debbie)

MINCEMEAT PIE

This is a two crust pie. Make dough for 8 or 9" pie
Use two cups of mincemeat, add 1 cup applesauce or cooked apples, cut up finely, ½ cup cream. Mix together put in pie crust. Put top crust on, pinch around the edge, make a few vent holes. . Bake 10 min. at 425deg. Reduce to 350 and bake 40 more min. Crust should be light brown. Serve with whip cream or ice cream.

MOCK MINCEMEAT

3 lb. Green tomatoes
5 lb. Apples
4 lb brown sugar
2 lb. Raisins (chopped)
2 Tbsp salt

1 cup Apple Cider vinegar
1 cup suet (½ lb. Chopped)
2 Tbsp ground cloves
1 Tbsp ground nutmeg

1. Chop tomatoes and drain well. Measure juice and add same amount of water to the pulp(do not add juice) Scald and drain off the liquid. Throw away the juice. Repeat this process twice.
2. Add the next six ingredients to the pulp and cook until clear.
3. Add remaining ingredients(spices) and cook until thick. It takes about an hour. Stir occasionally over med to low heat.
4. Cold pack for 10 minutes.

This was originally my Grandma Bearman's recipe and passed down to my Mom and Aunts.

The common procedure was to collect the green tomatoes that were still on the tomato plants in the garden, at the end of the season, to use to make the Mincemeat.

When the tomatoes were ripe and juicy, we ate lots and lots of them. My Grandma had a large garden and she had rows and rows of them. She had the small Italian and small yellow tomatoes aside from the big fat juicy red slicing ones. My brothers, boy cousins and I sometimes would go out to pick a few to eat and end up having a tomato fight. We all knew we could not get by with this at home but for some reason, Grandma's are different.

TOMATO PIE

This is a one crust pie. Put unbaked crust in pie pan.
Sprinkle 1/3 cup sugar around bottom and then sprinkle 1 Tbsp flour around bottom.
Peel and slice tomatoes to cover pie pan bottom. Sprinkle ½ cup sugar on top of tomatoes. Add a little cinnamon, sprinkle around tomatoes. Then sprinkle another ½ Tbsp flour over tomatoes.
Bake at 350 degrees until crust is light brown around the edge

Use very ripe tomatoes.
This was my Dad's favorite pie and my brothers liked it too.

MY PECAN PIE

2 eggs beaten	1 cup sugar
1 cup Karo syrup	2 Tbsp melted butter or margarine
1/8 tsp salt	1 cup pecans
1 tsp vanilla	

Mix ingredients together, add ing pecans last. Pour into Unbaked Pie crust. Bake in 400 degree oven 40 to 50 minutes. A table knife inserted in the top center of pie should come out clean. Cool before cutting. Good plain or with a dab of Cool Whip or Whipped Cream.

Pecan Pie

Aunt Nancy's Pecan Pie via her Aunt Audrey Dudgeon

PECAN PIE

2 eggs well beaten   ¼ cup butter or margarine
1 cup light corn syrup   1 tsp vanilla
½ cup brown sugar   1 cup pecans
¼ tsp salt
 Need one unbaked pie crust shell

Mix all ingredients but pecans well. Pour into unbaked pie shell. Sprinkle pecans over the top. Bake 40 to 50 minutes at 350 -375 degrees. You can use dark Karo corn syrup and granulated sugar for same results.

ROSY RED RHUBARB CAKE (more like a pie)

½ cup shortening   ¼ cup brown sugar
2 ½ tsp Baking Powder   2 cups flour
                            ¼ tsp salt

Cut shortening into dry ingredients like pie crust.
Add 1 Egg
¾ cup milk. Blend together and spread in bottom and up the sides of a 13X9x2" PAN. Cover with 6 cups of finely cut rhubarb. Sprinkle over the top the following;
Mix together: one 3 oz. Pkg Strawberry Jello (can use sugar free) 1 ½ cup sugar, ½ cup flour Add 6 Tbsp butter (in slices over top). Bake at 350 degrees for 50 min.
Cool before cutting.

My Mom's recipe …….Vera Springer

These are also from my mom and are they delicious!

STRAWBERRY PIE

2 Tbsp light Karo syrup	1 cup water
1 cup sugar	3 Tbsp cornstarch
3 Tbsp strawberry jello	1 Qt Strawberries

Bring Karao syrup, sugar, water and cornstarch to a boil, stirring constantly, until clear and thick. Then add jello. Can add a few drops of red food coloring if desired. Let cool.

Arrange berries (be sure they are cleaned and dry) in baked pie shell. Pour cooled glaze over whole strawberries. Covering well.
Chill. Serve with Whipped cream over the top.
 (optional) fruit can be slices and mixed with glaze and then put in cooled baked pie shell. Cover with Whipped cream to serve. Keep chilled.

The above glaze can be made to cover sliced fresh peach pie.
Substitute Peach Jello. Do not use red food coloring.

CRUST

Crust: 5 cups flour   1 egg broken in 1 cup
       2 cups shortening   fill cup with water
Cut shortening into flour, add egg & water to make dough. Pat into bottom of 8 to 9" pie shell. Bake at 400 degrees, 12 to 15 min. Cool well before adding fruit. A small amount of the cooled glaze can be added to the bottom of the cooled pie shell to keep it getting soggy before adding fruit.

APPLE PIE

5 or 6 large tart apples   peel, core and slice to make 4 cups
1 cup white sugar
1 tsp cinnamon
2 Tbsp butter
1½ Tbsp flour

This is a two crust pie,
Put sugar, cinnamon and flour in a bowl, mix together. Add the apples and coat them well.
Place in the unbaked pie crust, Slice the butter in small pieces and place over apples. Cover with top crust. Press edges together, cut a few air slits in top. Bake in Pre heated 425 degree oven for 10 minutes, then lower temp to 350 degrees, bake 30 to 40 min. more. Crust should be light brown. Cool to room temp before cutting. Can serve plain or with vanilla ice - cream.

FRESH PEACH PIE

4 Cups peeled and sliced peaches
1 cup sugar
4 Tbsp flour
2 Tbsp butter

This is a two crust pie. Put sugar, flour in bowl and coat peaches. Place peaches in unbaked pie crust. Top with butter cut in small slices. Place top crust on, press edges together, make a few air slits. Bake pre heated oven at 425 for 10 min. lower to 350 degrees for 30 to 40 minutes. Crust should be light brown. Cool to room temperature before cutting. Serve plain, with whipped cream or vanilla ice- cream.

BLUEBERRY PIE   or   BLACKBERRY PIE

4 Cups Blueberries, fresh or frozen
1 cup sugar
3 Tbsp flour
1 Tbsp butter

This is a 2 crust pie 8 or 9"
Coat berries with sugar and flour and place in unbaked pie crust.
Put the butter, cut in small pieces on top of fruit. Place top crust on pie. Press edges together.   Cut some air vents in top.
Bake in preheated 425 degree oven for 10 min. then reduce to 350 for 30 to 40 minutes. Crust should be light brown.
Serve with whipped cream or ice cream.

CHERRY PIE   Sour Cherries
4 cups fresh or canned sour cherries
 (if using canned, drain well and use only ¼ cup sugar and ½ cup juice from can)
If fresh use 1 cup sugar
1½ Tbsp flour
Mix fruit with sugar and flour, then put fruit in unbaked pie crust,
Cover with top crust. Press edges together. Make some air vents in top Bake in preheated oven 425 degrees for 10 minutes then reduce heat to 350 and bake 30 to 40 minutes longer. Crust should be light brown. Cool before cutting. Serve with whipped or ice-cream.

Hint: After top crust is put on, sprinkle some granulated sugar on it before putting in the oven.. Adds a little crunch and looks nice.
My Mom made a custard pie with cherries in it. I have never found a recipe for it, but if you do, it is very delicious.

PUMPKIN PIE

When I pulled all my recipes for pumpkin pie that I have collected for my over 50 years of marriage, I discovered there is a basic recipe and minor variations on Pumpkin pie. So here are two, one with sweetened condensed milk & one with evaporated milk.

PERFECT PUMPKIN PIE   (Prep time 10 min. serves 8)

1 15 oz. canned pumpkin (about 2 cups) Libbys
1 14 oz can sweetened Eagle condensed milk
2 eggs
1 tsp cinnamon   (Can substitute 2 tsp.
½ tsp ginger   Pumpkin pie spice for spices)
¼ tsp nutmeg
½ tsp salt   1 9" unbaked pie crust

Preheat oven to 425 degrees. Mix pumpkin, condensed milk, eggs, spices and salt together in medium bowl, until smooth. Pour into crust. Bake 15 min then reduce heat to 350 deg., bake 35 -40 more or until table knife inserted in pie center comes out clean. Cool. Serve with whipped cream. Refrigerate covered.

FAMOUS PUMPKIN PIE   (Prep time 10 min. serves 8)
2 eggs, slightly beaten   1 tsp cinnamon
1 ½ cups Libby canned pumpkin   ½ tsp ginger
¾ cups sugar   1/8 tsp. cloves
1 2/3 cups evaporated milk (15 oz can)   (can substitute 2 tsp
1 9 in unbaked pie crust   Pumpkin pie spice
                                           For spices)

Mix filling ingredients, stir until smooth. Pour into unbaked pie crust. Bake in 425 degree preheated oven for 15 min. Reduce heat to 350 and bake   approx 40 more min. Check with knife test.
Cool. Serve with whipped cream. Refrigerate covered.

Pumpkin pie

Marlo Ann

PIE CRUST

There are many variations on making pie crusts. The best hint I can give is to not work the dough any more than necessary, to keep it light and flakey. The recipe that I used and find the easiest, as I can always remember it, is very good, as follows.

3 cups flour	pinch of salt
1 cup shortening	1/3 cup ice water

Cut shortening into flour and salt, use medium size bowl until it is crumbly. Slowly add the water until you are able to form the dough into a ball. (You may not need all the water). The best way is to have all ingredients and equipment at the work station handy, and use your hands to work the dough.
Make a ball of the dough and place on a floured cutting board or counter. I put some wax paper down first, so clean up time is to gather the paper together and toss. Use only enough flour to be able to roll the crust out. Also, a seasoned rolling pin, flour it and roll the crust approx $1/8^{th}$ to ¼ in. thick, (so you can pick up to put in pie pan) Make crust 2 in., approx larger than pie pan. Place in the pan. If it is a single crust pie, then press around edge, 1 finger down, leave finger's width and then the finger down. Makes a decorative crust (on a two crusted pie, do this when pressing the two crusts together). If you do not have a rolling pin, get one. Until that time, take a wine bottle or something of a similar size and use to roll out the dough.

As a child, when Mom had scrapes of left over dough, she would roll it out in smaller pieces, put in a pie pan, sprinkle with sugar and cinnamon and bake it. What a treat, we loved it. I made this for my daughters and hope they have done the same.

Nancy Springer's PIE CRUST

Melt 2 cups lard (not hot)
      (I substituted 2 cups vegetable shortening)
Put in a large mixing bowl and add 5 cups flour. Mix well.
This dough can tolerate being handled.

Put 1 Tbsp vinegar, 1 Tbsp salt, one egg in a 1 cup measuring cup, finish filling the cup with milk. Add this to the flour mixture,
Mix well.
Chill or freeze before using. You can roll the dough out when it is chilled, making up crusts for Several pies. If you are not going to bake all the pies at the present time, can put rolled out crust in pie pan and freeze for a later time. Separate a top crust from a bottom one with wax paper before wrapping and freezing. Use metal pie pan to freeze.

Bake single pie crust in preheated 350 degree oven approx. 12 minutes or until light brown.

GRAHAM CRACKER CRUST

2 ½ Cups Graham Cracker crumbs
¼ tsp. Salt   ¼ cup melted butter
Blend ingredients together and pat into buttered pie pan. Chill 30 minutes before filling or bake at 375 deg. 8-10 minutes. Cool & fill

Flowers in my Yard

Marlo Ann

Salads

We all love salads and there are so many variations. If you find a good dressing recipe, you can use it on most vegetables. If you have some lettuce, and there are many kinds for a variation, just add some fresh vegetables cut up and there is a salad. But I do have a few that are really special. My mom made the best potato salad and I learned from her. Again, I repeat, ingredients can be adjusted to personal tastes.

Potato Salad, sliced eggs for presentation

POTATO SALAD

Boil 5 eggs, hard boiled, cooled and peeled (set aside)
Boil 6 medium russet potatoes (not huge ones) till done
When cool, peel and cut into small pieces, place in bowl.
Add 1 medium sweet onion chopped fairly fine
4 med. stalks celery cut in small slices (approx 1 cup)
Cut up 4 of the boiled eggs and add to potatoes.

In smaller bowl add approx 1 ½ cup Best Foods Mayo
1 tsp mustard (either classic yellow or grey Poupon)
1/3 cup sweet pickle relish
1 tsp salt   dash or two of pepper, a little of Mrs. Dash seasoning
Mix together and   add to the potato mixture. Should have enough
Mayonnaise mix to cover potatoes well. If not, add additional amount of Mayo and a little of the pickle relish juice.

Put the salad in serving bowl, slice the last egg (more if you wish) Place slices on the top of the salad, sprinkle with Paprika and garnish with some parsley.

BROCCOLI SALAD

Prep time 20 min.   Makes 6 ½ cups

Ingredients	Dressing
½ cup raisins	1 cup mayonnaise
1 cup peanuts	1/3 cup sugar
1 cup chopped red onions	2 Tbsp apple cider vinegar
4 cups broccoli flowerets	

Combine all salad ingredients in a large bowl. Combine dressing ingredients in small bowl and mix on salad when ready to serve.
(You may not want to use all the dressing, it will keep in fridge)

For a variety, chopped cauliflower or petite thawed frozen peas could be added. Also, crisp, broken up bacon or bacon bits.

SPINACH & STRAWBERRY SALAD
   This is from my good friend, Sharon Billings

Ingredients	Dressing
2 cups fresh baby spinach	½ cup salad oil
2 cups strawberries, sliced	¼ cup apple cider vinegar
½ cup minced red onion	½ cup sugar
1 tsp poppy seeds	1 tsp sesame seeds

Mix   salad ingredients. Add dressing right before serving. Makes lots of dressing, so do not use all at once. Keeps well in the refrigerator.

TAVERN DRESSING

1 onion chopped   ¾ tsp. Salt   ¾ cup vinegar
¾ cup chili sauce   ¾ tsp paprika   ¾ cup vegetable. Oil
¾ tsp celery seed   2 cups sugar.
Add one ingredient at a time and beat. Refrigerate. Makes 1 qt.

This is from Turkey Lake Tavern in Indiana, from Nancy Springer

MANDARIN ORANGE SPINACH SALAD

4 cups fresh baby spinach
2/3 cups thinly sliced mushrooms
1 ½ cups thinly sliced fresh mandarin oranges
 Or 1 can canned Mandarin orange segments
½ cups thinly sliced red onions
2/3 cups slivered toasted almonds

Gently toss all ingredients with a Balsamic Vinaigrette, especially an Orange Balsamic Vinaigrette, about 3 Tbsp

CRUNCHY PEA SALAD

Ingredients	Dressing
1 10 oz pkg. Frozen petite peas (thawed)	2/3 Tbsp lemon juice
	1 cup red wine vinegar
1 cup chopped celery	1 tsp salt
¼ cup green onion, (inc. green)	¾ tsp pepper
1 cup chopped macadamia nuts	1 Tbsp Worcestershire sauce ¼ cup
imitation bacon bits	1 tsp Dijon mustard
1 cup lite sour cream	1 glove garlic, smashed
¼ cup of Dressing	1 tsp sugar
	3 cups salad oil
Combine ingredients. Mix	Blend all seasonings then
Sour cream and ¼ cup dressing.	Slowly add oil. Blend.
Gently fold over ingredients	(Can USE for many
Serve WELL chilled	dressings. Refrigerate)

The above recipe came from Ruth Boyd, a long time friend.

When I first came to California, I had never tasted Avocados.   Ron's Mother made a salad with Avocado and that was how I thought it was used. When Ron was sent overseas to Korea, I lived with his parents, along with Debbie who was a toddler, for one year. His Mother was English and was a professional photographer and his Father made custom frames for oil paintings and unusual size items. This was totally different from my life on the farm, but we got to know each other very well and shared ideas. This is her recipe for Avocado salad.

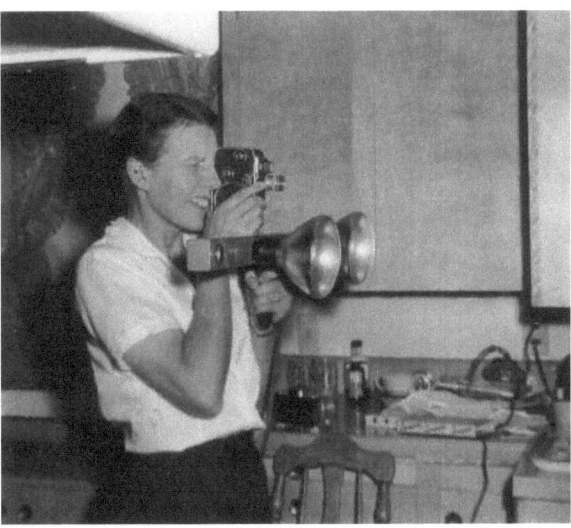

Ron's parents and baby Debbie

AVOCADO AND GRAPEFRUIT SALAD

½ head of Iceberg Lettuce   1 Avocado
1 grapefruit   ½ cup Mayonnaise

Break the lettuce in small pieces. Peel and cut the grapefruit in sections, Peel and cut the avocado in small pieces and add both to lettuce.
Gently stir mayonnaise over the above ingredients and you had a wonderful tasting salad.

HOT POTATO SALAD

This is a German potato salad and sometimes my Mom made it.

Cook about 6 medium sized potatoes, peel and cut in small pieces
Chop up 1 medium size onion and add to the potatoes
(Optionally can add 1 cup chopped celery)
Fry ½ lb cut up bacon till crisp
Add together and mix   1 Tbsp flour   1 egg, beaten
                        ½ cup water   ½ cup vinegar
                        ½ cup sugar
 Add the 5 ingredients to the bacon and let simmer for a few minutes. Pour hot bacon mixture over potatoes. Salt & Pepper to taste. Serve warm.

ORIENTAL SALAD

Ingredients	Dressing
½ head red cabbage shredded	1/8 cup sesame oil
½ head green cabbage shredded	¼ cup safflower oil
½ cup toasted, slivered almonds	½ tsp salt
3 Tbsp toasted sesame seeds	3 Tbsp apple cider vinegar
3 to 4 green onions sliced	
1 pkg. Vegetarian ramen noodles crushed	1 Tbsp sugar
Seasonings from ramen noodle pack	1 tsp pepper.
Mix all ingredients and stir in dressing	Mix dressing well.

COUNTRY SALAD

10 small plum tomatoes   (can use any small salad tomato)
2 or 3 cucumbers depending on size
2 small green onions
1 green Bell pepper (very colorful to use red & yellow also)
½ lb feta cheese
½ cup black olives'
Salt and pepper
Clean and cut up tomatoes in bite size pieces. Slice the cucumber. Mince the onions and peppers. Cut up the feta cheese. Place all in salad bowl, add olives and season. Add ½ cup oil, ¼ cup apple cider vinegar as dressing

CELERY SEED DRESSING

½ cup sugar   1 cup salad oil   1 tsp. Dry mustard
1tsp. Salt   ¼ tsp celery seed   1/3 cup vinegar
¼ cup grated onion. Mix in blender   Pour oil in slowly. Shake before using.
Good with Vegetables or fruit salad.

From Nancy Springer

DANDELION GREENS SALAD

After a long winter and no fresh greens, we looked forward to the first young dandelions to spring from the ground. My job was to take a bowl and paring knife and walk along the fence line rows and dig out a bowl of the dandelion greens. Bring them home and cut off the roots, then wash thoroughly. They had to be cut while very young and tender or else the taste would be bitter, long before the blooms came.

The salad dressing was the sweet sour dressing.
½ lb. Bacon, cut in ¼ "slices, fry till crisp (remove grease)
Add 2 to 3 Tbsp. Apple cider vinegar
1 Tbsp sugar   salt and pepper to taste
Pour over bowl of approx 4 cups greens, mix gently.
Add 2 sliced hard boiled eggs and mix again, gently.

DANDELION AND HOT POTATO DISH

The second way we fixed the Dandelions was with potatoes and it was the hot dish.

4 cups of dandelion green.
Cook ½ lb bacon, cut in ¼" slices, fry till crisp (remove grease)
Add ¼ cup vinegar
2 Tbsp sugar   Salt & pepper
Meantime: peel 4 or 5 potatoes medium sized, (if new potatoes just scrub well) Cut in small pieces and cook in large skillet, in small amount of water until tender. Add the bacon dressing to potatoes. When you are ready to serve, add dandelions to very hot mixture and stir together well. Do not cook the dandelions. I have bought commercial dandelions in the market but they are not as tender and sweet the early ones growing in the fields that I dug out as a child.

Here are some salads that my little girls wrote out for me, I can visualize their little hands helping me cook dinner.

CRANBERRY ORANGE RELISH
2 large oranges
4 cups fresh cranberries
2 cups sugar.
 Grind the oranges (remove all seeds) and the cranberries. Mix in the sugar and refrigerate. Great with your Turkey dinner.

TOMATO CHEESE SALAD

One tomato per person, cut in 4ths and placed on a lettuce leaf, on a salad plate. Spoon one large Tablespoon Cottage cheese (or more) in center of the sections, sprinkle some paprika on top. Serve

RASBERRY SALAD

1 small package of Rasberry jello
1 cup hot water
1 ten ounce package of frozen raspberries, partially thawed
1 cup applesauce

Mix together and refrigerate until set up
Then add topping before serving

TOPPING
1 cup sour cream
1 cup miniature marshmallows

Handwritten Recipes

Soups

The fun of making soups is adding ingredients that go well together and enjoying a hot bowl of soup on a cold day. I make a big pot of soup, as I keep adding more things to it, and freeze part of it. When we want a light meal, or are in a hurry or just want a bowl of soup, it is easy to defrost and serve.

Vegetable soup

VEGETABLE SOUP

If you have fresh vegetables you are in Heaven, as they make a terrific soup. A Beef bone for flavor, or vegetable broth or just browning onions in butter to a golden brown, and add from there. I make it in a crock pot normally, or my cast iron kettle.

Using 2 cups of broth, add a large can of tomatoes. Then add what vegetables you have. If you have frozen Vegetables, add 4 cups.
I add about ¼ cup of barley.
Slice 2 stalks of celery in small slices
1 carrot sliced small (if not using frozen vegetables slice up 2 carrots)
If not using frozen vegetables, add the following:
1 cup corn, 1 cup peas, 1 cup green beans.,
Add some water or tomato juice to make more broth and seasonings to taste,
When soup has cooked and vegetables are done, add a cup or two of cabbage, that has been sliced off the head ¼ in. thick and cut in 3 in. pieces. Cook for another 10 to 15 minutes.

Serve with crackers or a nice crusty loaf of French bread.

MINESTRONE SOUP

1 Large 14 ½ oz) can vegetable broth (or beef if you prefer)
1½ cup thinly sliced green onions or 1 cup minced onion
1 cup thinly sliced carrots
5 cloves garlic chopped
1 cup celery sliced very fine
1 large can Italian tomatoes (or just regular will be O'K)
1 16oz. can great northern white beans, drained (or 2 cups if cooked from dried beans)
1 16 oz. can kidney beans (do NOT drain)
2 cups green beans cut in 2 in. pieces (fresh, frozen or canned)
½ cup small shell macaroni or small pieces of spaghetti, uncooked
2 tsp. Dried basil
2 tsp. Dried oregano
2 tsp. Dried parsley
Salt & pepper to taste ¼ tsp approx. each
¼ tsp red chili pepper flakes or chili powder
1 cup water or enough to make nice amount of broth

Mix together in large pot. I use my cast iron Dutch oven usually and cook approx 30 to 40 minutes, slowly. (Can use crock pot but allow longer time to cook)
Serve into bowls and sprinkle Parmesan cheese on top. Can garnish with fresh basil. Serve with crusty French Bread or rolls

PEA SOUP

(Soak dried split peas overnight in bowl of water)

½ Tbsp olive oil
1 med. Onion chopped (1 cup)
4 cloves garlic, peeled & chopped
2 carrots, coarsely chopped about 1 ½ cups
1 stalk celery with leaves chopped
1 pound green split peas, rinsed and picked through
8 cups water
1 bay leaf
1/2 tsp dried thyme leaves or 1 Tbsp. fresh
1 tsp salt, black pepper to taste
(If you desire meat in the soup, it is good with ham or a ham bone for flavoring)

Heat oil in large kettle or Dutch oven, over medium heat. Add the onions and cook, stirring occasionally, until onions begin to soften and brown, add the garlic, carrots and celery, cook for 3 to 4 minutes, then add the split green peas and water and spices. Bring to a simmer. Cover tightly and cook for 1 ½ hours approx. Remove the bay leaf and discard. Soup should be thick and creamy, if too thick, add a little more water until a nice smooth consistency.

Is good served with crusty French bread.

FRENCH ONION SOUP

5 Large sweet onions, peeled and finely sliced
2 Tbsp butter
1 Tbsp olive oil
Heat oil and butter in large pot (I u se my cast iron Dutch oven)
Add the sliced onions and cook slowly, stirring often, until the onions are a deep rich golden brown. This is what makes the flavor. Can add 1 tsp of sugar to the browning onions, ½ tsp salt and a pinch of pepper. When onions are tender and rich brown, add 4 cups water and let cook very slowly 3 to 4 hours. (Can cook in crock pot if desired after the onions are browned). If too rich, add a little water.

Serve in soup bowl, add a small slice of French or sourdough bread and a thin slice or grated Parmesan on top. Heat in oven until cheese melts and then serve. (Be sure bowl is oven proof) Can be served with just the bread and individuals can sprinkle grated cheese on top to their personal taste.
Additional bread should be served with soup.

Marlo Ann

BEEF & BARLEY SOUP

This very simple soup was what I always wanted when I was sick.

Brown beef bones for stock or you can buy beef broth . Make lots of broth and add Barley to it, Approx. 3 cups broth to 1 cup Barley. A few fresh Vegetables can be added, carrots & celery, peas, Salt & pepper to taste. Cook slowly , 2 to 3 hours. Some quick cooking Barley is now available.

NOODLES

Before we go into making noodle soup, I have to explain what all was involved. First of all it would be either a holiday or a Sat. afternoon when Mom had time to make the noodles. We would have to, unfortunately, kill a chicken on Sat. evening, as that would be Sunday's dinner. We had to do all the preparing the chicken for eating and that is too gross to go into here. Mom would then make the noodles.

3 egg yolks	2 cups flour	3 Tbsp cold water
1 egg	pinch of salt	(makes 1 pound)

In a fairly large bowl whip up the eggs, add the salt and with your hands work in the flour. The dough should be real stiff. Divide into three balls, Cover and let rest for a few minutes while you prepare the counter or board to roll out the dough. Cover the bread board (or where you are going to be rolling the dough) with flour. If you put waxed paper down over the board it will be a easier clean up. (Dampen the area before putting down the wax paper and it will not slide). Also put flour on your rolling pin. Take one ball of dough and roll out as thin as possible. Then place the whole rolled out piece on a piece of waxed paper that is placed over the back of a kitchen chair, leave it there to dry. Repeat with the other two balls of dough. After about 2 hours when the noodles feel dry, take them, one piece at a time, back to the floured board. Cut it into strips about three inches wide, stack the strips and slice off very thin 1/8 to $1/4^{th}$ in. the noodles. The width will depend on if you want very thin or wide noodles, they will be larger when cooked. Thin noodles are best. Repeat this on all three pieces of dough. When all the dough has been sliced into noodles, let them set on the floured board, and turn them a few times, to let them dry well. A well dried noodle will last almost indefinitely, and they freeze very well.

Our goats and chickens, our pets

NOODLE SOUP

You can cook a whole small chicken and use the broth for the soup, or the bony parts, like wings, back & neck for the broth, and fry or roast the rest of the chicken.

In a fairly large pot bring salted water to a rolling boil and slowly add the noodles. Boil rapidly until noodles are tender. About 10 to 15 minutes, depends on how thin you rolled the dough out and how thin you sliced them. Taste them to see if they taste cooked.

Once you get the hang of making the noodles, you can determine how many you want for a meal. For soup you can add the noodles into the broth directly and when they are done, you can add the chicken. If you want to use them as a side dish, they of course you won't need as much water or broth.

To be safe, the first time or so, you can always cook them in salt water and then pour the water off and add the cooked noodles to your broth. Just like spaghetti. Mom knew exactly how much to make. She also knew just how to cut them. It is funny, but the men would comment and compare on how good the ladies noodles were.

THRESHING DAY

A little story about Threshing Day. That was the day when the farmers came to help each other thresh their oats or wheat. Now they use combines and it is nothing compared how it used to be done. That is a whole story in itself. On Threshing day the women cooked a beautiful noon meal. Put out the white tablecloths and good dishes and silver. The men came in, after washing outside in tubs that were provided to wash their face and hands. They were served a banquet. Each hostess would try to outdo the others as to the food and elegance of dinner. If it was a long day, an evening meal was served, the women would buy cold cuts and various foods that were only for special occasions, to be served.

Most farmers had a summer kitchen. A small building that had a kerosene stove for cooking in the summer, as well as a table and chairs. Both kitchens would be busy, as it would be quite warm outside when the threshing was done. After all the meals were eaten, the men ate first, the kids often at a second table ate second and the wives ate last. Then it was clean up time with dishes to be done. There was no running water, We would carry buckets of water to be heated so the ladies could wash stacks and stacks of dishes.

We kids loved it, as we ate very well on those days. We got to see and play with the other kids that came with their parents. In the evening when the work was done, we were allowed to play on the haystack. That was really fun.

At the time I was very young, farming was done with horses. It was a lot of back breaking work. My Grandpa's farm was a much larger farm than ours and we would help them work in the fields. The oats and the wheat were cut with a farm implement called a binder. It was pulled by a team of horses, Grandpa at the reins. It would cut the grain and bind it in bundles. This was a step up from cutting by hand with a scythe. Anyway after the binding was done, we would take the bundles and stack them in a round in groups of four bundles and then the fifth one on top of the stack. That was to help keep the rain out, as there were showers occasionally. The farmers all wanted to get the grain thrashed before rain came, a big worry.

If the grain was wet it would mold, so it was important that the grain be cut at the correct window of time, and then left to dry a short period of time and then the grain separated from the stalk, which is what threshing was. The farmer's crop would depend on his eating and paying the bank.   There was one farmer in our area that had a Threshing Machine and he was a busy man .

When they raised corn, Mom and Dad would often go out at night when it was a full moon and husk the corn from the stalks. They would toss the corn on the ground and in the daylight hours we would walk the rows with a horse & wagon, with us kids throwing the corn in the wagon. The corn stalks would then be cut by a large knife and bundled up and stacked up in the fields. It was used for fodder, or feed for the animals. Again, this work was dependent on the corn being ready and the weather co-operating. No time to waste.

Our farmhouse

Wild Roses and Childhood Memories

I can remember being so sick one day, I was home from school in bed and the upstairs of our house had no heat, ice froze over in the glass of water Mom had placed by my bed. She was out working in the field. My older brother helped very much, he and Mom made a good team. My Dad had a job in the factory in the city, so he was not there during the daytime. The point of the story is, I could not complain that I was alone in bed and sick because when my parents were young, they had to go out in the fields and work anyway. No one could use the excuse of being sick to not help do necessary work. We had it easy compared to our parents.

We grew pumpkins and melons in the corn rows and in the summertime had lots of watermelon or musk melon, in the winter, pumpkin pie. That was one of our chores, to hoe all the stalks of corn and cut out any thistles when the stalks were young.

Now heavy equipment goes in and does this work. Tractors were such a wonderful blessing for the farmer, if he could afford it. We have watched TV shows, such as "Little House on the Prairie" and they had to walk behind a horse pulling a plow to plow the fields. I can still see my Dad doing that to plow our garden, when I was very little. He really did not like farming as much as my Mom did. When we got our tractor my brothers did the field work, I brought them cold lemonade. I was glad for a change that I was a girl!

Marlo Ann on Tricycle

Aunt Sally would make the best Potato Soup. This was sent to me by Nancy Springer. It is very similar to Aunt Sally's.

POTATO SOUP WITH RUFFLES

1 potato   1 small onion and ½ cup water and cook till tender.
(Cut the potato in small pieces and mince the onion.)

Ruffles: Mix 1 egg in 1 cup of flour.

Sprinkle the Ruffles mix over the potatoes & onions
Mix & stir, add two cups milk and ½ cup butter. Cook till flour and egg mixture is cooked, about 10 minutes. Season to taste.

MILK SOUP

When we had lots of milk from the cows and the price of milk was low or the cupboards were bare or there was a reason to use up lots of milk, Mom would make the above soup but no potato, just lots of milk. We didn't like it but ate it anyway. That and some crackers were dinner.

Many times our before bedtime snacks would be crackers and milk or bread and milk. Break some saltine crackers up in a bowl, put a spoon of sugar in and pour milk over. If no crackers, do the same with white bread. If you are hungry, it tastes pretty darn good.

Indiana Cornfield

Wild Roses and Childhood Memories - 91 -

Main Dishes

Stew

Marlo Ann

CABBAGE ROLLS

1 Cup ground beef, cooked	½ tsp pepper
1 Finely chopped onion	1 tsp salt
2 tsp chopped parsley	1 cup canned tomatoes
½ cups cooked rice	6 large cabbage leaves

Mix meat, onion, parsley, rice, salt and pepper and 1/3 cup of tomatoes. Wash head of cabbage well, remove 6 leaves with care and pour boiling water over them. Spread each leaf with meat and rice mixture, roll up tightly & fasten with toothpicks or tie with string.
Grease a baking dish, place cabbage rolls in it. Pour rest of tomatoes over them. Cover and bake in 350 degree oven for 45 min.

This recipe was given to me years ago when we belonged to the Trojan Boat Cruising Club, Betty Forbes was the hit of all the pot lucks with her…….FARMER STYLE SPARERIBS

2/3 Cups ketchup	2 cups Crushed pineapple	
1 tsp garlic powder	2 Tbsp brown sugar	2/3 cups water
1 very finely chopped onion		
2 Tbsp vinegar	4 to 6 Farmer style ribs	
2 Tbsp Worchester sauce	(all pork meat)	

1st brown the ribs and get rid of the grease. While ribs brown, sprinkle garlic salt on them. Mix the rest of ingredients together, really well. Put all but ½ cup sauce on ribs and bake at 350 degrees for about 2 ½ hours. Take lid off and pour on rest of sauce, bake another 15 minutes or so. Ribs should be really tender. Good served with rice or baked potato and salad.

Girls boating (From left to right) Debbie, Laurie, Lisa, Kathy

Most people today know about Hamburger Helper, it came out in the 70's and then I started to hear the term again in the past year or so. Before there was a packaged mix, which consisted of measured amount of macaroni and spices, you still have to supply the hamburger, there was…

CHILI MAC

1 lb lean ground beef
1 small onion, chopped
1 chopped green bell pepper
In large skillet, brown meat and add onion & pepper

Then add, cover and simmer about 15 minutes, stir occasionally
 1 (8-oz) package elbow macaroni or small shell macaroni
1 (16-oz) can kidney beans, include liquid
2 (8-oz) cans Tomato sauce
1 cup water
1 tsp. Chili powder   1 tsp. Salt   1 tsp. Oregano

Then top with 1 cup grated cheddar cheese. Heat till melted.
This recipe can be cut in half.

When we would go to visit Ron's parents and his Mother fixed dinner for all of us, she would make her recipe similar of the above and it was called…..   GOOP

Goop was made like Chili Mac except she used cooked Pinto beans and did not have the Bell pepper in it. It was cooked much longer, stirred periodically. Instead of melting cheese on top, we put sprinkled Parmesan cheese on top. Parmesan was nick-named stinky cheese by our youngsters. We still call it that.

Serve with some rolls and butter and small salad, a filling meal.

PIZZA

Back in the late 1940's Pizza became popular, at least with our family. Our Uncle Dewey became our Pizza man. He always was trying new things. Chef Boyardee came out with a pizza mix and he would make it, with his own variations. There were no local pizza parlors, there may have been a few in the city of Fort Wayne, but we would never have gone to a restaurant. We loved Uncle Dewey's pizza. After I was married and had moved to California we lived on very tight budget, prepackaged food was not in that budget. I did use Bisquick and started to experiment with my own Pizza recipe. The girls loved it and we would have Pizza parties. I made our Pizza even after the girls were teenagers and we were feeding boyfriends, as well as our family and friends.

PIZZA CRUST

1 cup Bisquick   2/3 cup water
1 cup all purpose flour

Mix Bisquick & flour with water to make dough. Grease bottom of round pizza pan or metal cookie sheet. Dust lightly with flour.
Place dough in middle of pan and roll out dough thin, with a crust around the edge. May need to use some flour to roll out dough. I have a small pizza dough roller. Can use small rolling pin or bottle.

INGREDIENTS

1 small can tomato sauce   spread out over crust
Add the ingredients that you enjoy on pizza as follows:

½ lb. Ground meat, browned and in small pieces
1 cup Mozarella cheese, grated   1 cup sliced salami
1 cup cheddar cheese, grated   1 cup ham & pineapple
1 cup Parmasan cheese, grated   bell peppers, some hot ones
1 cup diced small mushrooms   various vegetables.

Season with Italian seasonings before adding cheese. Bake 400 degree oven for 30 minutes, when crust looks brown, pizza bubbly.

SPAGHETTI SAUCE

Brown approx. ½ pound of lean ground beef and 4 sweet Italian sausages (sausage optional but adds lots of flavor)
Chop up 1 onion and some fresh garlic and brown with meat.

Add 1 (15 oz). can Tomato sauce
     1 (15 oz) can cut up tomatoes
     1 (6 oz) can tomato paste dilute with 1 can water

Season with a pinch of dried oregano & basil, salt & pepper and one dried red pepper or pepper flakes if desired. you can also use Spaghetti seasoning.
    If you are making lots of sauce, add a jar of Spaghetti sauce to the above. Simmer for 30 minutes or so, to get flavors blended.

Cook approx ½ small package spaghetti noodles (8 to 10 oz)

Serve with a salad and some French bread, makes a great meal, especially with a nice glass of red wine.

LASAGNA

1 pound lean ground beef	Sauce:
1 small onion, minced	2 cups canned tomatoes
2 garlic cloves, minced	1 large can tomato sauce (2 cups)
2 cups cottage cheese	1tsp. Oregano
½ lb. Swiss cheese, cut in small squares	1 tsp Basil
	½ tsp salt, ¼ tsp pepper
½ lb. cooked Lasagna noodles	Or you can use
½ cup grated parmesan cheese	1 qt. jar prepared Spaghetti sauce

Brown the meat, onions & garlic. Add to sauce. In the bottom of a shallow baking dish, 10X5"
Cover bottom of dish with a small amount of sauce, then a layer of cooked noodles, a layer of cottage cheese, a layer of Swiss cheese, then sauce. Repeat layers ending with noodles, cover with remaining
sauce. Sprinkle Parmesan cheese on top. Bake at 350 degrees for 20 to 30 minutes, till hot & bubbly.

Marlo Ann

MEAT LOAF

1 Pound lean ground beef	2 Tbsp ketchup
2 eggs	¼ chopped onion
12 saltine crushed)	¼ tsp salt & pepper
1 8oz can tomato sauce	

 Mix all ingredients and put into a loaf pan, or pat in a loaf shape in small baking pan. Use 4or 5 additional crackers, smashed small and sprinkle over top of meat. Squeeze a squiggle of ketchup across top of crackers, on top of meat loaf . Bake in a 350 degree oven for one hour.

Bake a potato for each serving and let bake while meat loaf is baking. Fix a vegetable and a salad to go along, for a healthy meal.

Meat Loaf, vegetables, and melon. A healthy meal.

GREEN BEAN CASSEROLE

White Sauce

1 ½ Tbsp butter	melt butter in small sauce pan over low
3 Tbsp all purpose flour	heat, stir in flour Cook 1 to 2 minutes stirring with a
3 to 4 Tbsp Ranch Style Dry Salad mix	whisk constantly, stir in milk, keep stirring, bring to boil, cook 1-2 min.
¼ tsp. Pepper	till thick, Stir in Ranch dressing & pepper. Set aside.

1 ½ cups sliced mushrooms
2 cloves garlic, minced
4 pounds fresh green beans- cooked till tender
1 cup bread crumbs

Preheat oven to 350 degrees. Spray skillet with Pam (or grease) and heat. Add onion and garlic, simmer for 2 to 3 minutes till tender. Set aside, add Mushrooms to onion mixture, cook another few minutes.
Combine all ingredients with green beans and white sauce in a 1 ½ qt. Casserole. Sprinkle with bread crumbs. Bake uncovered about 20 to 30 minutes, Until bubbly and crumbs browned.

SWEET POTATOES

Bake 3 to 4 Sweet Potatoes or Yams. Depends on how many you plan to serve. Bake till tender., approx 1 hr. at 350 degrees. Cut tips and put in a pan to keep oven clean. Cool and peel
Cut into pieces, approx 2 ½" size. Place in casserole dish, put small pat of butter on each piece, sprinkle with brown sugar, you can add a few spoons full of marmalade if desired, Heat uncovered in oven till Hot, 15 to 20 min. Remove from oven and add some marshmallows to top. Return to oven until marshmallows melt and are lightly brown.

BEEF STEW

½ pound stew meat or small chuck roast cut in 1" cubes
3 medium sized potatoes peeled and cut in 6ths.
1 medium sized onion cut in approx. 1" pieces
3 large carrots cut in 1" pieces
2 large stalks of celery cut in ½ " pieces

In a Dutch oven or heavy 3qt size pan, heat approximately
2 Tablespoons oil to brown the meat. Coat the meat pieces with flour (approx. 1/3 cup) Salt & pepper and brown in the hot oil. Watch so it does not burn, stirring until all sides are browned. The browned floured meat will make a nice gravy. When meat is browned, cover with water and let simmer. Cover with lid and simmer approx. ½ hour. (Simmer is cooking on low heat). If necessary add a little more water. Add rest of vegetables and enough water so they can cook. (covering the vegetables half way) Cook on low heat until carrots are done. Season with some Parsley or Mrs. Dash seasoning, which I often use. Season to taste. You can add button mushrooms for a variety. This is good served with a salad and hot French bread. Will serve four persons.

A favorite German dish my Dad loved was POTATO PANCAKES. It was lots of work to make and you had to eat them right away. This is one time my Dad would help Mom cook, as it was his way of making them. We had to help grate the potatoes, which was a job no one wanted, The grated potatoes will discolor, it doesn't affect the flavor but doesn't look as good, so have everything ready when you start so the grated potatoes don't have to sit. You can make the pancakes and keep them warm in the oven until they are all cooked but it is best to serve immediately. Remember, we had a wood burning stove and it was a little more difficult to control the temperature.

POTATO PANCAKES

4 medium potatoes
1 egg (lightly beaten)
2 Tbsp flour
1 Tbsp. cream
1 tsp.salt. A pinch of pepper
Butter to cook pancakes

Wash and peel potatoes and grate with fine grater. Drain off all the liquid that has collected, squeeze grated potatoes, with paper towels to get all the liquid out. Add egg, flour, salt & pepper. Place 1 Tbsp butter in large skillet or griddle, put approx ¼ cup of potato mixture in hot skillet, per pancake. Press to flatten. Cook gently until brown and turn to brown other side (approx. 4 to5 min) Use approx. 1 tsp butter per skillet of pancakes.

We ate them served from the skillet to our plate and covered with room temp. canned pears & juice as syrup. It was a rare treat. We made them in batches, so sometimes it took awhile for us all to get satisfied.

Another Potato Pancake we would make was to use up left over Mashed Potatoes. It would depend on how many potatoes were left over, usually not many.

MASHED POTATO PANCAKES

2 cups mashed potatoes   1 Egg
1 Tbsp. melted Butter
Mix together, put in a greased heated skillet,(use oil or butter) to brown the pancakes in.

My Dad and second youngest brother, Denny
and
My oldest brother Gene and youngest brother, Allan

Marlo Ann

There used to be a restaurant in Orange County, in Southern California that served the best corn. It was called Gulliver's. Our Eldest daughter, Debbie acquired the recipe for……

GULLIVER'S CORN

4 packages frozen corn or 1 large 20 0z bag
2 cups whipping cream
1 cup milk
1 tsp. Salt
6 Tbsp sugar
Pinch of pepper

Mix all ingredients together and bring to a boil, Simmer for 5 minutes.
Mix 2 Tbsp melted butter and 2 Tbsp flour. Add to mixture and stir till corn mixture is thickened.
This makes a lot, recipe can be cut in half. Or enjoy leftovers.

RON'S MEAT LOAF

Ron normally did not cook but now and then he would get ambitious about cooking, the little girls giggled and just loved it. It made me happy to see them all so excited. Of course he did this with great fan fare and no one could watch him cook. It was a big surprise. Of course great Chef's don't clean up. Ouch! It was great. The food was good too and I did not have to cook it.

1. 2 cups unbroken Jack LaLane soya crackers
2. Smash crackers
3. Roll sleeves up
4. 1 Sweet onion, dice small
5. Also cry a lot
6. Place onion in dry mix and mix around
7. Chop up ½ cup dates and add to mess
8. Add 1 Tbsp Brown sugar
9. Add ¼ cup ketchup and mix well
10. Add 4 ounces of crushed pineapple to mess
11.. 2 eggs add to mess
12. 1 ½ lb. Ground chuck, add to mess and mix thoroughly
13. Dash salt and pepper
13. 1 tsp soy sauce and mix
15. Put meat in meat loaf pan
16. Sprinkle top lightly with brown sugar and ¼ cup crushed pineapple

Bake 1 hr. in 350 degree oven.
I take no responsibility for this recipe. Ron dictated it to the girls, Debbie, wrote it out and saved it for posterity.

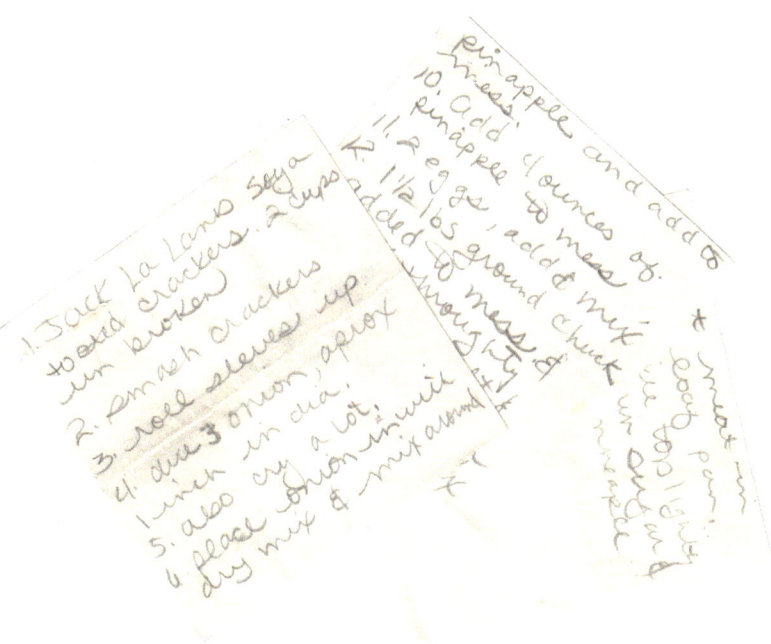

Sweet & Sour Pork

1. Cut up one pound of lean pork in small cubes
2. Heat 2 Tbsp oil in a skillet
3. Toss in pork cubes and fry until well browned.
4. While meat cooks cut 2 medium size sweet onions in quarters
5. Cut 1 green bell pepper into strips
6. Remove any excess grease, add vegetables to pork and cook Until limp.
7. Add 1 can (2 cups approx.) crushed pineapple. Stir
8. Add 2 Tbsp vinegar   Stir
9. Add 1 Tbsp soy sauce, stir
10. Add ½ tsp salt, stir
11. Mix 1 Tbsp cornstarch with 1 cup water until smooth. Slowly stir into meat & vegetables. Bring to a boiling point and reduce heat to very low and cook about 1 hour or till meat is very tender. Stir occasionally. Makes approx. 4 cups. Serve with rice

ZUCCHINI & CHEESE

4 or 5 small zucchini, thinly sliced about 3 cups
1 Tbsp. Olive oil
½ tsp. Salt   Dash of pepper
¼ cup grated Parmesan cheese
Put Zucchini, oil and seasoning in a skillet, cover and cook slowly about 5 minutes. Uncover and cook turning slices until barely tender, about 5 minuters. Sprinkle with cheese, Toss and serve.

ZUCCHINI AND TOMATOES

4 or 5 small zucchini, sliced about ¼ "thick
1 medium sized onion sliced thinly
1 can tomatoes, or 4 or 5 peeled fresh tomatoes, cut up
¼ tsp salt -   dash of pepper
(Optional 1 small bell pepper cut up in small strips)
Put all ingredients in skillet with lid or corning ware, cover.   Place on heat and cook slowly about 10 minutes, until tender.

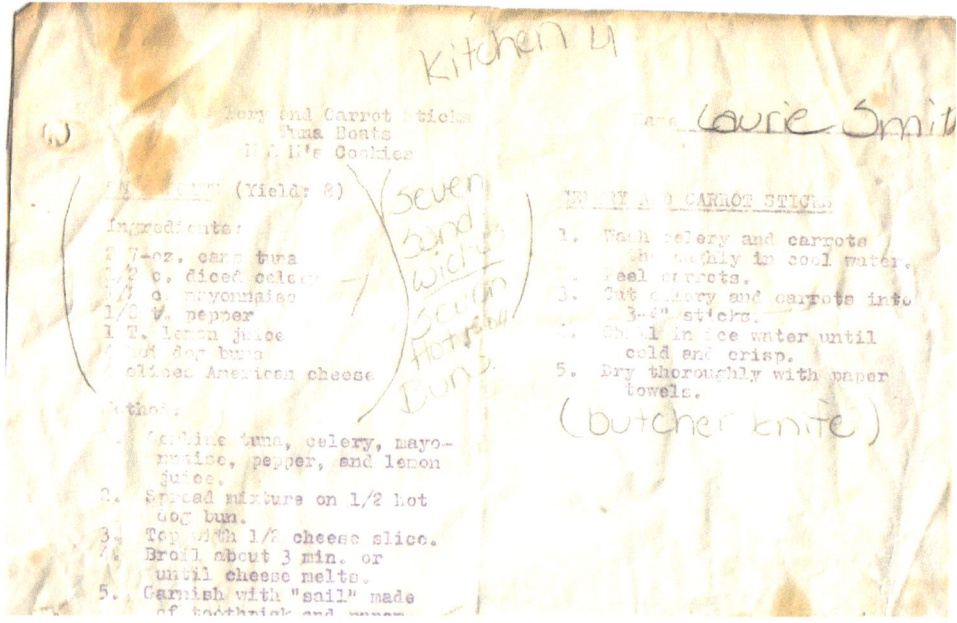

When the girls were old enough to use the stove they learned how to cook. As they got a little older, they would work in pairs and each two girls had to fix dinner one night a week. These are some of their recipes. It was a great help.

ZUCCHINIS WITH VELVETTA CHEESE

7 or 8 medium to large zucchinis
1 cup Velvetta cheese, cut in small cubes
½ to 1 Ortega green chilies, chopped

Peel zucchinis, slice and cook until tender. Drain, then add cheese and chilies. Stir until cheese is melted. Season with salt and pepper

American cheese can be substituted or cheddar cheese.

As Laurie was the youngest, her cooking was the easiest in her choices. With the younger child working with an older sister, we had a nice variety of foods. These were some of Laurie's. She was 6 or 7 years old.

HOT DOG CASSEROLE

1 ½ package of Hot dogs, sliced in half (length wise)
1 chopped onion
1 package cheddar cheese, grated (6 to 8 oz.)
1 large can cooked tomatoes
Layer in a deep Casserole dish, hot dogs, a handful of cheese and a handful of onions. Layer again etc. till out of food. Cover with the tomatoes.
Bake for 20 to 25 minutes at 400 degree oven

TUNA BOATS

2 7 oz cans tuna
½ cup diced celery
½ cup mayonnaise
1/8 tsp pepper
1 Tbsp lemon juice
4 hot dog buns
4 slices American cheese
Combine ingredients and spread on ½ of bun, top with cheese. Broil about 3 minutes or until cheese melts.
Garnish with small paper sail on a toothpick.

CAMPER STEW
½ pound hamburger, browned and added to one can of Campbells ABC soup.
Cook together until soup is hot.
(This is a revised version by good ole Mom)

Lisa and Kathy's interest in cooking was more involved in elaborate dishes, being a few years older helped. They would work together for some fine meals.

Here are some of the recipes they prepared.

CHILI RELJENO

2 Small cans of whole green Ortega chilies
1 lb. Sharp cheddar cheese
½ lb Jack cheese
4 eggs, beaten
2 Tbsp flour (heaping)
½ tsp salt
1 large can evaporated milk
1 large can tomato sauce (15 oz)
Remove seeds from chilies, wash off and drain on paper towels.
Grease 9X13 casserole dish. Line bottom with split chilies,
Grate cheese and sprinkle over top of chilies
Beat eggs, flour, salt and milk together and pour over cheese.
Bake at 350 degree oven for 35 minutes. Remove from oven and pour tomato sauce over top. Return to oven and bake another 5 minutes or until tomato sauce is bubbly in the center. Good with Mexican food.

CLASSIC CHICKEN DIVAN

2 10 oz packages of frozen broccoli spears or approx. 1 lb fresh broccoli.
½ cup whipping cream
¼ cup butter or margarine   3 Tbsp dry white wine
6 Tbsp all purpose flour   6 half chicken breasts, cooked
2 cups chicken broth   ¼ cup grated Parmesan cheese
Cook broccoli and drain. Melt better, blend in flour, add ½ tsp salt & dash of pepper,
add chicken broth, cook, stirring till mixture thickens and bubbles. Stir in cream and wine,
Place Broccoli crosswise in 12 X 7 ½ X 2" baking dish,. Pour half the sauce and the cheese over top, then add chicken. Add rest of sauce. Sprinkle with additional Parmesan cheese. Bake at 350 degrees for 20 minutes or till heated thoroughly. Then broil just till sauce is golden, about 5 minutes. Makes 6 servings.

CHICKEN & OLIVES DEVILLE

2 eggs	2 Tbsp. flour
2 large boneless chicken breasts, halved	1 ½ cup milk
½ cup fine dry bread crumbs	1/3 cup sliced
3 Tbsp butter or margarine	stuffed green olives
½ cup sliced almonds	dash garlic powder
4 med potatoes, pared, sliced and boiled.	2 Tbsp parsley

In small bowl beat eggs, Dip chicken in egg mixture, coat with bread crumbs. In med skillet, heat 1 tbsp oil, add chicken, slowly cook until brown & done, about 20 min. Place chicken on heat proof platter, keep warm in oven.

Almond olive sauce

In same skillet, melt butter, add almonds, sauté', stirring until golden brown approx. 2 min. Stir in flour till smooth. Cook over low heat, stir constantly till bubbly, slowly add milk, and stir in olives, parsley and garlic. Cook over low heat till mixture thickens, stirring constantly. Add salt & pepper. Pour over chicken. Garnish with potatoes, parsley and olives. Serves 4.

One of the nicest recipes that the girls gave me is as follows:

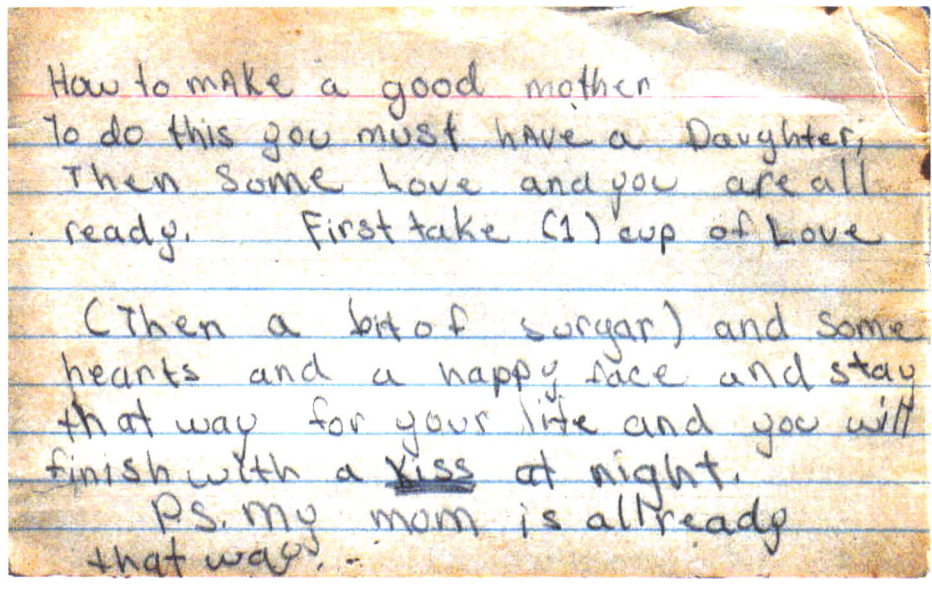

How to make a good mother
To do this you must have a Daughter,
Then some Love and you are all
ready. First take (1) cup of Love
(Then a bit of sugar) and some
hearts and a happy face and stay
that way for your life and you will
finish with a kiss at night.
P.S. my mom is allready that way.

Marlo Ann

HOW TO MAKE A GOOD MOTHER

To do this you must have a daughter, then some love and you are all ready.

First take (1) cup of Love
(Then a bit of sugar) and some hearts and a happy face and stay that way for your life and will finish with a KISS at night.

p.s. My Mom is already that way.

Oh how I cherish that recipe card.

    My Mother was a good Mother, and she had so much love in her heart. She suffered many pains, but never complained. I remember her sewing my clothes, as I had to wear dresses. She made me clothes all through my school years. My Uncle Dewey would give her suits he no longer would wear at his business office and she would take them apart to make skirts and vests, or jackets. Late at night she would be sitting at her sewing machine. Early on it was a treadle machine before she had it converted to electric.
    Not only did she sew for me, but for anyone who needed anything. In her later years, long after I was in California, she worked in a nursing home. She had so much compassion for the patients, she would bring home their clothes and mend them. She made alter cloths for our church alter and I know they were still using them years and years after her death. They were beautiful. We had hand crocheted doilies for our tables, and edgings on our pillow cases. She made beautiful quilts. She was an amazing woman.

My Mom sewing

When my darling husband brought me to California, he introduced me to a whole world that I had no idea existed. I love the ocean, to walk along the beach in the surf is the one thing I have missed so much now that we live in Northern California and away from the ocean. The variety of food was amazing. I had never had a Taco. I love tacos. To be able to have fresh fruits and vegetables all year round was wonderful. You must remember this was over fifty years ago, I learned how to make Mexican dishes like Enchiladas. When we would make trips back to Indiana to visit my family we would bring tortillas, avocados, taco sauce, jack cheese, all the makings for Mexican food. I would make tacos for everyone. The Indiana crowd loved them too.

A family visit back to Indiana
(from left to right) Marlo Ann, Laurie,
Debbie, Ron, Lisa, Kathy

Tacos

Brown 1 pound ground beef, break into very small pieces
Add 2 Tbsp. Ketchup
    1 Tbs. Chili powder
Mix together and keep warm on stove

Cut up very fine 1 or 2 tomatoes (depends on size)
2 or 3 green onions very fine, including green part
Grate 2 cups cheddar cheese
2 cups finely sliced head lettuce
Put these ingredients in separate small bowls

In skillet heat small amount of oil and add one tortilla, when it is hot, turn over, when it is hot both sides remove and place on a paper towel. I have a plate and towels torn in half, to place tortilla on and cover both sides, then fold over. Cook the amount of tacos you will be serving this way. Keeping them covered with paper towels, help to keep them warm. When amount tortillas cooked, fill with the ground meat mixture. Serve and let each person put his own condiments in. Serve with taco sauce, Red & Green.

Enchiladas
Beef
Mix in a medium size bowl: ½ cup grated cheddar cheese
1 small can ground or sliced black olives
5 small green onions or 1 med onion, minced
Brown 1 pound ground beef, 1 clove garlic and add to the above mixture. (Can add chili beans if desired)
Sauce: 1 can chili con carne, ½ cup water 1 small can tomato sauce. Heat sauce in skillet. When hot, dip corn tortillas in sauce
And place in baking dish. Fill tortilla with the meat mixture, fold tortilla over both sides. Filling will be in the middle. (Makes approx. 8 enchiladas) Repeat Procedure I usually use an approx. 10 X 5 ½ in baking pan. Cover tortillas with remaining sauce. Sprinkle grated cheese on top. Place in 350 degree oven for 15 to 20 minutes.
Variety options: I sometimes use jack cheese grated on top.

Chicken: Use ½ cup grated jack cheese. 1 small can ground or sliced black olives, 5 small green onions or 1 med onion, minced. Shred 2 cooked chicken breasts or use one (12.5 oz) can of chicken breasts, For the filling. Complete as the above recipe.

Shrimp: Make as for chicken, but cut up 2 cups of cooked, de-veined shrimp or 2 cans bay shrimp or cooked fresh bay shrimp.

You can use a prepared canned Enchilada sauce if desired for the sauce.

Good served with refried beans and rice, or tacos. I use canned refried beans and heat with grated Jack Cheese on top.

For rice, cook white rice per directions but add mild salsa for a spicy taste. 1 cup rice, 2 /½ cups water, ½ cup mild salsa. Cook rice approx 20 minutes or till done.

FISH TACOS (story)

It is hard to find fish tacos like what you find in Baja, Mexico. Partly because they use fresh catch of the day and when they run out, they quit making them. There is one little shop in the town of Loreto, in Baja. We always tried to get there early, as they serve the best Fish Tacos. It is family owned and they work the small taco stand. The food is always fresh and delicious. We certainly would eat our fill when visiting in Mexico.

FISH TACOS

Use very fresh fish, Halibut, Red Snapper or a fish of your choice.
 Again it depends on the amount of servings you will be making, so if you cut two strips of fish that are approx. 3 inches long and 1 inch wide for each corn tortilla, you can approximate how much you will need.
Fish: Prepare the fish by cutting in approx 3 inch lengths, about 1 inch wide. Dip in a beer batter and fry them crispy in oil.

BEER BATTER….. Take an egg and whip it up, add Bisquick or similar product (a cup will go along way) Add Beer, enough to make a constancy to coat the fish. (The cook gets to drink the rest of the beer while preparing the tacos.) It makes a nice crisp coat. I don't deep fry but you can, I put just enough oil in a skillet to brown the fish on both sides, being careful not to break the pieces up.

Have ready, cabbage that is sliced very thin. Cut a head of cabbage in half and start slicing from the cut half. You use cabbage instead of lettuce.
Avocado, that is mashed and add ¼ cup mayonnaise, 2 Tbsp. Sour cream, mix it all together well. Makes a creamy avocado sauce
Cut up tomatoes in small pieces. You can use salsa or taco sauce.
Put the fish in a warmed tortilla, flour or corn as you prefer, add the cabbage and sauces,
Don't have beer? Dip fish in egg and coat with flour or Bisquick.

Taco Dinner

LILACS

No, not to eat. This morning as I walked outside to feed the chickens and goats, I saw the lilac bush had brought forth blooms. When I was little, we had three huge lilac bushes at the side of our lane, in front of the farm house. I loved those bushes when they would be in bloom, their fragrance filled the air.

I would pick huge bouquets and we would have the best smelling house around. As I was a little older and cleaning the house was my job, on a Saturday I would like to start early and clean the full two story farmhouse, top to bottom. Mopping the kitchen floor last, I would then pick bouquets of flowers to fill the rooms.

When we were very small, I was Mom's helper. We got a bath in a round wash tub, in the winter it was in front of the cook stove. She would then mop the kitchen floor at night with the bath water. In the summer, if we were going someplace, we filled the wash tub and let it sit out in the sun to warm up to got our baths. Sometimes it was just to cool off. No sprinklers for us, we had to pump and carry the water.

One year, Mom was able to drive to Ft. Wayne and buy some things for the house. It was a needed day for her (I can now understand) I was about 9 years old and left in charge of my two little brothers, one 6 and one about 3. I can't remember where my older brother was, he was usually working in our fields or at our neighbors. I cleaned the house and gave my brothers their baths. We had a Watkins Salesman that made the farm routes to sell his wares, come by and I sat through his whole spiel, just as my Mom had always done. (I learned later that he had told the neighbors all about it when he visited their farms). When my Mom got home from town, with the car full of items, she was very pleased to have clean children and a clean house. My reward was a story book .

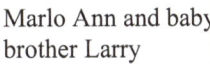
Marlo Ann and baby brother Larry

Marlo Ann

There are now growing in my yard many of the various trees, plants and flowers that my Mom had. It brings back so many memories. We have iris, a ground cover we called "Snow On the Mountain" which my catalogue calls "Bishop Weed" that came from the farm. We have Dogwood trees, as we had them in our woods. Bridal Wreath, as Mom called Spiraea, is now in bloom, we had a huge bush in front of our house. Mom would always pick a bouquet on Memorial Day and we would put it on the grave of her first born, another little girl, Flora Jean. We have Wild Roses, Climbing Roses, Hydrangeas, and of course Lilacs.

I hope Mom is looking down and smiling at our Home. I am sure she is happy that her home has stayed in the family, my younger brother, Larry and wife, Pam, live on the farm, it is now their home. They have done wonderful remodeling and it is always a joy to go back and visit.

My Mom had a large "Snowball Bush" that she was so proud of. I have one in my yard not, not as large as hers. It seemed to always be in the way of the farm equipment and she would try to protect it as much as she could. On my last visit to the farm, the bush was very healthy. I know she would be happy about that. I can sit at my computer and look out the large sliding glass door and see my "Snowball Bush", it brings back such happy memories and love for Mom.

(Bottom to top) Kenny, Marlo Ann, and Gene in front of the Bridal Wreath bush (Spiraea).

The current farmhouse in Indiana

Jellly and Jams

Growing up we always had homemade jelly and jam, preserves, relishes and quite a variety.

My Dad loved tomato preserves.

This is the recipe my Mom gave me, many years ago.

Marlo Ann

TOMATO PRESERVES

(Use recipe on Certo package if using Certo. Otherwise:

Peel and take out seeds of ripe tomatoes (as many seeds as you can) Squeeze out as much of the juice as possible. You want the bulky thick part. Take equal amounts of sugar and tomatoes. Cook until thick, as desired, (15-20 minutes) Watch closely because it burns easily. Stir constantly.

I made these for my Father-In-Law years ago and used the Certo recipe. He was from Ohio and grew up on the same type cooking as I had.

When we bought our house in Long Beach, California, we had a wonderful apricot tree in the back yard. We loved those apricots and I would make lots of Apricot Jam,

Our eldest daughter, Debbie, got the bright idea of making a trade. She stopped the Ice-Cream Man one day and asked if she could trade some apricots for ice-cream bars, for her and her sisters. At five years old we were impressed. So was the Ice Cream Man, as they made that trade for several days.

Debbie and Apricot Tree

Lisa and Kathy with our dog Sallie. "We would rather have ice cream"

APRICOT JAM

Using very ripe fruit, I use 4 cups prepared fruit, 3 cups sugar.
(Fruit washed, the pits removed and any blemishes cut out, the fruit cut in smaller pieces,.) If necessary add a little water to keep from burning. With very ripe fruit, usually the juices would form soon enough and water not necessary. Start with a lower heat and stir constantly until juices form and sugar is melted. Then cook at a higher temperature and let boil rapidly until it is thick. Stir constantly. You can test for doneness with a thermometer or an old fashioned way, set the pan off the burner. Have a small cold metal pan or heavy saucer, and drop a little cooked fruit on it and stick in the freezer or fridge for a minute or two to see if it will jell or if still runny. Cook until it will jell. Pour into sterilized jars. If you use Certo, follow those directions. It is usually much less work involved.

When we moved to Northern California, we had lots of wild blackberries. I started making Blackberry Jam. Black Raspberry had always been my favorite as a youngster. We would go out in the woods and along fence rows to pick them at the farm. At our home in Newcastle, California, we have a creek nearby and lots of wild blackberries. Picking the berries the first few years, it was a great adventure for the grandkids to help me. The first couple years there was a raft we could use on the creek and the kids thought that was fun. They out grew that adventure. Soon, due to the scratched arms and legs and mosquito bites, along with lack of time, I lost all my berry picking helpers. It is now my Motherly duty to go out and pick those berries, alone. Family, neighbors and friends get jam for Christmas.

I use Certos and the recipe on their instructions sheet.

Marlo Ann

My good friend and neighbor, Ione, gave me this recipe.

STRAWBERRY FIG JAM

3 cups fresh cut up figs (cut in small pieces)
1 6oz package of fat free or sugarless Strawberry Jello
3 cups sugar
Mix Figs, Jello and sugar all together, bring to boiling point.
Cook on medium heat, boiling and stirring for 5 minutes.
Immediately remove from heat and put in sterilized jars.

It is fun to experiment making different kinds of Jams. I have made some that didn't succeed and some that turned out perfect. If your jam comes out a little runny, it is wonderful on French Toast. Ice Cream toppings can also be made from jams that are runny.

If someone says they have a tree that is full of fruit and want to find a home for it, help pick it. Nothing is better than fresh fruit from the tree. It can be frozen and jam or jelly can be made at a later date. When the blackberries are ripe in August and September and the temperature is 103 degrees, the berries get cleaned and measured and put in the freezer. By measuring them before I freeze them, they don't have to be completely defrosted when I start my jam makings.

I use Corning ware to cook in and wooden spoons to stir. Begin by sitting out all equipment, Sterilized Jars & lids, a shallow pan, with water to place my clean jars in, upside down, on low heat. Have A plate to put the jars on when it is time to fill them. Have hot pads, dish cloth, timer, jar lids, a pair of tongs, cup to fill the jars, a spot to put them,   Then, start to cook your jam.

Be sure to read the instructions on the Certos package.

Beverages

In the 60's and 70's we were in the Sun Tea era. We still make sun tea but at that time our daughters were old enough to drink tea and share ideas on making it. We spent a lot of time in the desert and drinking lots of fluids was essential.

Bengal tea was my favorite brand and it doesn't seem to be around anymore. Other teas will do. My husband drinks Lipton tea everyday, so I always make that for him. There is such a variety in my tea drawer; it is a big decision as to what kind to choose from.

A refreshing drink in the Grape Arbor

SUN TEA

Put three tea bags in 1 quart jar. Fill jar with cold tap water, Seal jar and set in the sun for approx. 6 hours. (remove the tags from bags or be sure they are left to hang outside jar. Bring in and remove tea bags, refrigerate to cool and enjoy.

RUSSIAN TEA
¼ cup instant tea
1 cup Tang
½ tsp. Cloves
1/3 cup Lipton ice tea mix with lemon and sugar
½ cup sugar
Mix together and store in a jar. Use 3 tsp to 1 cup boiling water. Very good as iced tea drink. Amount may very per personal taste.

MINT TEA
Add a sprig of mint to a freshly brewed cup of tea and let seep.

CINNAMON TEA
Add a cinnamon stick to a freshly brewed cup of tea and let seep.

WASSEL
1 gallon of apple juice or apple cider (warmed)
1 cup Brandy
1 orange with cloves stuck all around it
Cinnamon stick to stir

Put orange in punch bowl, add brandy and then apple juice.
Stir with cinnamon stick.
Can be put in a crock pot to stay warm or placed on a warming tray.

The following recipe is due to telling our adult children about my first cocktail. It was a cold winter night and we were just of age to legally drink, both of us having birthdays in December. We went out to dinner and my husband bought me a Brandy Alexander. I loved it. Since we never really drank cocktails nor went to bars, my choice of drink (should the occasion arise) was always the same for a long time. I felt so grown up and cosmopolitan to order a Brandy Alexander! My children all laughed at me, in loving fun, I must add.

BRANDY ALEXANDER
2 oz cream
1 oz Brandy
1 oz Cacao liqueur (dark)
Nutmeg powder for garnish
Pour liquor and cream into a ice filled shaker and shake. Strain into a cocktail glass and garnish with nutmeg.

MEXICAN CHOCOLATE

This is one that Laurie wrote years ago. Her Dad and I changed the ingredients around a little to satisfy our taste. You have a choice of the original recipe or our version.

3 Tablespoons of Cocoa
3 Tablespoons of sugar
2 cups of milk (cold)
½ cup water
1 egg
1 tsp vanilla
Pinch of cinnamon and nutmeg

Add all ingredients and mix in blender till frothy.

> Mexican Choclate Recipe
> (Serves 8)
>
> 3 tablespoons of Cocoa
> 3 tablespoons of sugar
> 1 quart of milk
> 1 cup of water
> 1 teaspoon of vanilla
> 1/8 of a teaspoon of Cinnamon
> 2 eggs
> 1/8 of a teaspoon of nutmeg

My two younger brothers are much younger than myself. They are in-between my age and my daughters. They came to California to visit, with my Mom when Laurie was little, about three years old.. Disneyland had been open in Anaheim for only a few years. So we all made our first trip to Disneyland (or Lislyland) as Laurie pronounced it.   WE ARE GOING TO LISLYLAND!!!!

The Family ready to go to Lislyland

My younger brothers loved the ocean as I do and for the first time, they had Seafood. So I will include a few Seafood recipes, for Shrimp. They enjoyed shrimp very much, especially after they learned they did not have to eat the tails.

Boiled Shrimp

It will take a large pot, at least four quart to boil the shrimp in. It will depend of course on how many you are cooking. The shrimp need to come to a rolling boil. To the pot of water you can add a prepared mix called Crab Boil, or put in your own spices. I will use Thyme, Basil, Oregano, Garlic, Chili powder, A pinch of each when I cook up a two pound bag of shrimp. Normally you buy it already de-veined and de-headed. We have bought whole shrimp and it is much more work. Also, the large shrimp are the best.

When the water comes to a boil, put the spices in and then the shrimp. They should just come to a rolling boil and turn pink and are done. Don't overcook. Immediately spoon out with a slotted spoon or pour into a colander to drain.

We learned about eating seafood when visiting New Orleans at Mardi Gras. We spent a week with a friends and their family. We had the traditional New Orleans foods and it was marvelous.

Marlo Ann at Marti Gras

In New Orleans, family style, they put the bowl of cooked shrimp in the center of the table and you serve yourself, the faster you eat the more you get. The table is covered with newspaper and by the time you are done, it is full of shrimp shells. Wad of the newspaper and toss. Dishes are done!,

To take off the tail, pinch where the tail begins and it will pull right off. Dip in Tartar sauce and enjoy.

Tartar Sauce #1

½ cup ketchup
1 Tbsp Mustard
1 tsp. Minced onion (optional)
½ tsp lemon juice
Can add a tiny bit of Horseradish if desired

Tartar Sauce #2

1/ 2 cup mayonnaise
1 Tbsp. Dill pickle relish
1 tsp. Minced onion

Mix together. Relish and onion can vary depending on personal taste.

Tartar Sauce #3

½ cup mayonnaise
¼ cup ketchup
1 Tbsp. Minced onion
1 Tbsp. Sweet pickle relish

Mix together. Again amounts of relish and onion can vary depending on personal taste.

I will serve rice with Shrimp and a green salad. Some crusty French bread and you have a feast.

Any left over shrimp can be served as a Shrimp Cocktail.
Cut the shrimp into thirds, cut some celery up fine and onion minced. Put in Shrimp cocktail glasses or a small bowl, cover with cocktail sauce or the #1 Tartar Sauce (which is like cocktail sauce)
Squeeze some lemon juice over it and enjoy. Serve it very cold.
Left over shrimp can also be added to a green salad. Again cut in thirds, if you have large shrimp, and it is delicious with lettuce etc.

NOTES OR EXTRA RECIPES

About the Author . . . .

Marlo Ann was born and raised on a farm in Indiana, the second oldest child with five brothers. After graduation from High School and a trade college, she met and married her husband, Ron.

At the time Ron was in the Air Force and his home was in Southern California. They moved to Long Beach, California and raised their four daughters.

She worked with her husband in his insurance office until they retired. It was a busy life, raising children, working and always working on home improvement projects. The family always came first and recreation was a family affair. Their activities included boating and motorcycle riding in the desert. Everyone worked together and played together.

After retirement, Marlo Ann and her husband moved to Newcastle, Ca. a rural area in Northern California. Retirement has not slowed them down. They have developed their two acres in the country to a beautiful park atmosphere. In their spare time they both enjoy boating, motorcycle riding and traveling. Family still comes first, she and her husband celebrated their 50th Wedding Anniversary in 2004.

This is Marlo Ann's first book, although she has had articles published about some of their many adventures.